ROBIN HAMBLETON

CITIES AND COMMUNITIES BEYOND COVID-19

How Local Leadership Can Change
Our Future for the Better

With a Foreword by Marvin Rees

BRISTOL
UNIVERSITY
PRESS

First published in Great Britain in 2020 by

Bristol University Press
University of Bristol
1-9 Old Park Hill
Bristol
BS2 8BB
UK
t: +44 (0)117 954 5940
e: bup-info@bristol.ac.uk

Details of international sales and distribution partners are available at
bristoluniversitypress.co.uk

© Bristol University Press 2020

British Library Cataloguing in Publication Data
A catalogue record for this book is available from the British Library

ISBN 978-1-5292-1585-4 paperback
ISBN 978-1-5292-1586-1 ePub
ISBN 978-1-5292-1587-8 ePdf

Cover design: blu inc, Bristol
Front cover image: Commission Air / Alamy (aerial view of Bristol
looking north with Brandon Hill Nature Park in the foreground)

Contents

Lists of Figures, Tables and 'Innovation Cameos'

About the Author

Robin Hambleton is Emeritus Professor of City Leadership in the Faculty of Environment and Technology at the University of the West of England, Bristol and Director of Urban Answers. An expert on urban innovation, city management and local governance, he was the founding President of the European Urban Research Association (EURA) and was also Dean of the College of Urban Planning and Public Affairs (CUPPA) at the University of Illinois at Chicago. Author of numerous books on public leadership and civic innovation, his last book was *Leading the Inclusive City: Place-based innovation for a bounded planet* (2015, Bristol: Policy Press).

Acknowledgements

Writing a book in ten weeks is not possible without a great deal of help from colleagues, friends and family. I thank Marvin Rees, Mayor of Bristol, for writing the Foreword and I thank Arturo Flores for writing the Innovation Cameo on Mexico City that appears in Chapter Six.

I have benefited from stimulating conversations with many scholars and practitioners, as well as very helpful comments on drafts of various chapters. My sincere thanks go to: David Ader, David Barclay, Richard Bolden, Nevin Brown, Christine Cheyne, Simon Cowley, Jamie Darwen, Wulf Daseking, Andrea Dell, Bas Denters, Laura de Vito, Lars Engberg, Valeria Fedeli, Arturo Flores, Aaron Hawkins, Mathew Jellings, Marta Lackowska, Jim Longhurst, Alan Macleod, Helen Manchester, Ali Modarres, Jacob Norvig Larsen, Thom Oliver, Ges Rosenberg, Ed Rowberry, Greg Schrock, Annabel Smith, Andy Street, Richard Stren, David Sweeting, David Towell, Ignazio Vinci, Bob Whelan and Karsten Zimmermann.

Bristol University Press has, as always, provided friendly, helpful and creative support to me as an author. In particular, I would like to thank my editor, Emily Watt, for her encouragement and wise advice, and to the whole team for arranging for this book to be published in next to no time.

This book could not have been written without the loving support of my family. Special thanks to Pam, the wisest and most supportive person I have ever met.

Foreword

Robin Hambleton inducted me into the understanding that the political challenge we face today is not down to a shortage in the supply of clever people coming up with new policy ideas. We have plenty of ideas. The political challenge we face today is also about the structure, machinery and tradition of our model of governance.

It's a model that systematically withholds power from towns and cities across the United Kingdom and concentrates it in Whitehall and Westminster. In doing so, it undermines the leadership of people who must live with the consequences of the decisions of central government politicans, and puts it into the hands of place-less power, people and organizations, who have no real grounding and no connection to the places about which they are making decisions.

The challenge of being a directly elected mayor, trying to deliver for the people of Bristol who elected me, but with so many of the powers and resources I need being controlled by distant offices and people, has been a source of immense frustration. It undermines our ability to be a dependable partner to other organizations in the city, undermines our ability to plan, and undermines our ability to flex our local understanding of challenges and opportunities and then act with the speed and innovation they require.

This is a story repeated by mayors and local authority leaders across the UK and around the world, as evidenced in the proliferation of national and international city networks. There is a growing recognition that on local issues, such as housing delivery and transport solutions, to global issues such as climate change and migration, the current model just isn't delivering. Its distance and turgidity create a high risk of putting out ideas that are bright but locally inappropriate, while blocking new sources of insight.

It's in this context that the COVID-19 pandemic, as Robin points out, presents us with an opportunity. The virus, the lockdown and the economic depression have been testing all our systems – from education, food and public transport to criminal justice, electoral politics (our local elections were deferred from May 2020 to May 2021) and our plans to tackle climate change. We have an opportunity to take stock of what we have become, where we are vulnerable, and where we are resilient, and to use that knowledge as a basis to reconceptualize and rebuild our model of governance.

The sobering reality is that we have tasted these opportunities before, following the World Wars, the cold war, the global financial crisis, the climate emergency. The status quo has proven to be very adaptable and very resilient. This is why I welcome Robin's thoroughly hopeful approach, built on an understanding that 'there is no going back' and an invitation to an exciting new future.

Marvin Rees
Mayor of Bristol

ONE

No Going Back

Introduction

The COVID-19 pandemic has already had a devastating impact on the world. Billions have had their lives disrupted and, by 1 July 2020, over ten million people had been infected and over 500,000 people had died. It is a safe prediction that, by the time you read this the figures will be much worse.[1] Other pandemics in the past have killed more people – for example, the horrendous Spanish flu of 1918.[2] But, reflecting the fact that we now live in a highly interconnected world, the COVID-19 virus set an unenviable world record in no time at all. It became the first virus to spread across the globe in a matter of a few short weeks.

Moreover, COVID-19 presents an ongoing threat, and it will almost certainly continue to do so, even after a vaccine is discovered. The gravity of our current predicament has led to many voices, as in 1945 at the end of the Second World War, pleading 'never again'. A central claim of this book is that the COVID-19 pandemic, while it is awful and merciless in every respect, provides all of us with a remarkable opportunity to engage in a radical rethink. We need to ask the question: after COVID-19, what kind of future do we want for ourselves, for our children, for our grandchildren and for subsequent generations?

Profound political choices now present themselves. Some believe that the best strategy is to roll back the clock to 2019, to revert, somehow, to the kind of world that existed shortly before this new, and lethal, virus emerged. Others take the view that the COVID-19 pandemic raises fundamental questions that need to be addressed. They ask: is it wise to believe that continued exploitation of people and the planet provides the right lodestar for modern societies? It may seem idealistic but perhaps now is the time to think through why the world is in such a bad place and, equally important, to share ideas on how to co-create a rather different world – one that recognizes that we are all interconnected.

In this opening chapter, I introduce themes that will be explored in more detail in the rest of the book. After a discussion of living under lockdown, I consider the possible objectives of a post COVID-19 recovery. A central claim of this book is that societal flourishing and future development will depend on people and organizations working far more closely together, and that *the key driver for this societal change can only be local.*

Around fifty years ago, grassroots, environmental campaigners adopted the slogan 'Think globally, act locally'. They were ahead of the curve in urging people to consider the health of the entire planet, while also taking action to improve society in their own communities and cities.[3] It must be gratifying for those early campaigners to see that schoolchildren across the world now learn about this way of thinking as part of their education, and many young people, as well as older people, are putting this learning into practice.[4]

Many city mayors and local leaders across the world are now actively implementing various kinds of 'Think globally, act locally' strategies. More than a few are demonstrating that bold collaborative leadership can access all kinds of community-based problem-solving capacity, and that local initiatives really can make an important difference to the quality of life.[5] Put simply, place-based leaders can tap into local energies and passions that are not available to distant national governments. COVID-19 has demonstrated that local communities are jam-packed with remarkably resourceful people. Local activists and leaders have responded with extraordinary care and compassion to the needs of others. We need to build on this foundation of solidarity in the period ahead.

It may seem unduly pessimistic to suggest that, right now, we need to start preparing for the *next pandemic*. Uncomfortable as it may be, the argument I present in this book is that modern societies now face a *range* of fiendishly complex and really serious public hazards. COVID-19 is a global catastrophe but, unfortunately, it is not a one-off. Pandemics have happened before and will happen again, and other alarming societal challenges also now present themselves for our urgent attention. Top of the list is global warming – it represents the ultimate test, as it threatens the future of human life on the planet.

History and science tell us that there will be more pandemics in the future. It follows that, as we design our post COVID-19 strategies, we need to develop much more effective arrangements for anticipating and coping with complex threats of whatever kind. This means that we have to improve the way we govern ourselves, and this is the central message of this book. The good news is that we can choose to do this. Moreover, across the world, there are many splendid examples of high-quality leadership and governance at international, national and local levels.

This chapter introduces some concepts relating to local power, the meaning of place and the nature of civic leadership. As we know, COVID-19 is not the first disaster to hit the world, and I include a short section, towards the end of the chapter, on the lessons we can learn from how societies have coped with previous calamities.

Living under lockdown

Many countries introduced lockdowns, or 'stay at home' orders, to reduce the spread of COVID-19 in early 2020.

Indeed, the disease led to the largest number of lockdowns ever implemented in world history. These 'stay at home', or 'shelter in place', orders have varied in detail but, taken as a whole, they represent the most far-reaching curbs on personal freedom we have ever seen. The abrupt imposition of lockdowns has brought out the best and the worst in us.

On the downside, there have been outbreaks of selfish, even hostile, behaviour by some people. Stories of shoppers rushing to supermarkets, pushing past others in efforts to buy excessive amounts of particular goods – for example, toilet rolls, paper tissues, hand sanitizer and the like – appeared in the news in many countries. On the upside, the lockdowns have created an enormous upsurge in social solidarity, with a spectacular increase in the number of people providing help and assistance to neighbours and needy groups of various kinds.

Paulo Giordano, an Italian physicist and author, has written eloquently about his experiences of lockdown in Rome in early March 2020. He explains how fear can make us do strange things. For example, he has a friend who is married to a Japanese woman. They live close to Milan and have a five-year-old daughter: 'Yesterday, mother and daughter were in the supermarket and a couple of men started yelling at them, saying it was their fault, they should go home, back to China'.[6] Giordano explains that 'they' are, of course, not to blame at all for the contagion; that, indeed, no specific group is to blame. Rather, his analysis shows that we are all culpable because of the way we have exploited the planet in an unforgiving and thoughtless way for several decades. Evidence to support this claim is presented in Chapter Two, where I discuss the emergence of the COVID-19 pandemic.

Giordano brings mathematical insights to his study of the pandemic and shows how, in a contagion, we rediscover that we are all part of a single organism: 'In times of contagion, therefore, what we do or don't do is no longer just about us. This is the one thing I wish for us never to forget, even after this is over.'[7]

Tobias Jones, a British author, expresses a similar insight:

> The penny has dropped that wellbeing isn't individual but social. We are not actually independent at all, but dependent. We can make each other sick and we can try to make each other well. We've understood that a healthy community isn't merely human, but also its soil, its water, its air.[8]

Jones offers a critique of market ways of thinking, of which more in a moment, and hopes that lasting good will come from the insights we have gained from collaborating and helping each other during these various lockdowns.

Is it still the economy, stupid?

In 1992, James Carville, a strategist working on Bill Clinton's successful US presidential campaign, came up with a memorable phrase: 'The economy, stupid'. The US was experiencing a recession at the time, and Clinton was able to use and adapt this phrase to very good effect during his imaginative campaign, not least because many citizens were worried about their jobs. Clinton defeated incumbent Republican President George H.W. Bush in a convincing victory.

Some commentators take the view that COVID-19 has rewritten the political script, and claim that 'it's not the economy any more, stupid.'[9] The bold measures taken by many nation states, including the extensive lockdowns, suggest that many political leaders have, indeed, prioritized public health measures and saving lives over economic considerations. In some countries, there have been intense political arguments between those who believe that public health priorities should always hold sway, while others claim that an indefinite freezing of the economy will have unwelcome public health – as well as adverse economic – consequences. In truth, some of these debates oversimplify. Wise political leadership recognizes that a healthy life for citizens and economic prosperity for society are two sides of the same coin. Returning people to work after a lockdown can be expected to have health benefits as well as economic benefits. Similarly, keeping people safe and well has economic benefits.

An important question, often left out of these debates, concerns what kind of economy do we want to develop when we recover from the COVID-19 pandemic? Some aspire to a return to a form of 'small state' capitalism, a world in which private interests dominate, particularly the interests of the very wealthy and gigantic companies, and that the conventional measures of economic performance should be retained. Others take the view that the COVID-19 catastrophe demonstrates that the avaricious pursuit of unbridled self-interest has shown itself to be a flawed approach, and that a new kind of economics – one that is guided by sound ethical, social and environmental principles – is now needed. The good news is that the public enthusiasm for developing a new sense of direction, as well as improved ways of measuring societal wellbeing, have grown significantly in recent years.[10]

Joseph Stiglitz, winner of the Nobel Prize for Economics in 2001, advocated striking a sensible balance between government and the market over thirty years ago. In several books he has exposed the intellectual flaws in so-called 'free market' ideology.[11] Stiglitz demonstrated that 'market fundamentalism', the belief that markets lead to economic efficiency, was not based on any evidence and that government leadership is critical in shaping economic and societal outcomes.[12]

Michael Sandel, the well-known political philosopher, in his acclaimed book *What Money Can't Buy*, takes the argument a step further. He shows how the global economic crisis of 2008–09 did more than cast doubts on the ability of markets to allocate risk efficiently. The crisis and the global economic convulsions that have followed in recent years have prompted a deeper sense of unease, a feeling that markets have become detached from morals and a broader sense of public purpose.

Sandel notes that, for many, the solution is to rein in greed, to insist on higher standards of probity in the banking industry, and to enact sensible regulations that will prevent irresponsible financial practices in the future. His major insight, however, is to recognize that such an approach is insufficient. Sandel argues that, while excessive greed played a major role in the financial crash, something more troubling was actually happening:

> The most fateful change that unfolded during the past three decades was not an increase in greed. It was the expansion of markets, and market values, into spheres of life where they don't belong … We need a public debate about what it means to keep markets in their place. To have this debate, we need to think through the moral limits of markets. We need to ask whether there are some things money should not buy.[13]

In my 2015 international book on how to develop inclusive city leadership, I built on Sandel's critique of modern society and argued that place-based leaders and local activists can play a vital role in highlighting the moral limits of markets.[14] More than that, place-based leaders can draw attention to other highly prized values, for example community, solidarity, generosity, caring for others and caring for the planet. The important role of local leadership in helping societies to recover from the trauma of COVID-19 will be explored in subsequent chapters. Before embarking on this quest, we should consider where we are starting from and ask: how much power do people living in particular places have anyway?

Place-less power and place-based power

COVID-19 is, of course, a global calamity. However, at the same time it is not so much a single phenomenon as a multitude of specific outbreaks affecting different localities and communities in very different ways. As we will see later, while the steps taken by national governments to respond to the COVID-19 challenge have dominated the headlines, it is the case that thousands of cities and localities across the world have played, and are continuing to play, an enormously important role in responding to the crisis and in helping societies to recover. Local leadership has the major advantage of being able to tap local knowledge and understanding. Moreover, civic leaders, in and outside the state, are uniquely well placed to support and orchestrate local community-based efforts to meet the needs of diverse vulnerable groups and to invent new ways of doing things.

Unfortunately, place-based leaders across the world are up against a malign force, one that has seen a spectacular growth in the last thirty years or so: place-less power. By place-less power, I mean the exercise of power by decision makers who are unconcerned about the impacts of their decisions on communities living in particular places. The forces of globalization, which have resulted in a remarkable growth in the number of multinational companies operating on a global basis, have provided the engine for this expansion in place-less policy making, and the consequences for social, economic and environmental justice have been dire.[15]

When exploring how elected local governments and other place-based actors might respond to societal challenges, it is important to understand the potential constraints on local political action. It is naive to believe that elected local leaders are free agents, able to respond directly and compassionately to the views and priorities expressed by their citizens. On the contrary, various powerful forces shape the context within which civic leaders operate. These forces do not erase the possibilities for local leadership. Rather, they place limits on what local leaders may be able to accomplish in particular countries and localities at particular moments in time. Figure 1.1 provides a simplified picture of the four sets of forces that shape the world of place-based governance in any given locality.

Figure 1.1: Framing the political space available to local leaders

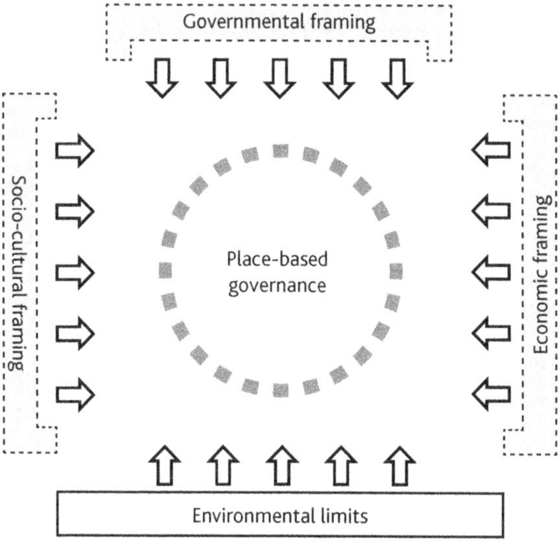

Source: Hambleton R. (2015), p 114

At the bottom of the diagram are, what I take to be, the non-negotiable environmental, or planetary, limits. The scientific evidence on climate change suggests that ignoring the fact that cities and local communities are part of the natural eco-system is irresponsible, and failure to pay attention to environmental limits will store up unmanageable problems for future generations.[16] This side of the square is drawn with a solid line because, unlike the other sides of the square, these environmental limits are non-negotiable.

On the left-hand side of the diagram are socio-cultural forces – these comprise a mix of people (as actors) and cultural values (that people may hold). Here we find the rich variety of voices found in any city or locality. The people of a given city or locality will have different views about the kind of place they wish to live in, and they will have differential capacities to make these views known. Some, maybe many, will claim a right to the city.[17] We can assume that, in democratic societies at least, elected leaders who pay little or no attention to these local political pressures should not expect to stay in office for too long. Expression of 'citizen's voice', to use a phrase deployed by the famous economist Albert Hirschman, will see them dismissed at the ballot box.[18]

On the right-hand side of the diagram are the horizontal economic forces that arise from the need for localities to compete, to some degree at least, in the wider marketplace – for inward investment and to attract talented people. Some writers argue that, owing to local resource deficits and the need to maintain a competitive position, cities have become dependent on higher levels of government and private investment for survival.[19] On this analysis, localities become ever more dependent on external forces, effectively helpless victims in a global flow of events. However, various studies have shown that, contrary to neoliberal dogma, it is possible for civic leaders to bargain with business.[20]

On the top of Figure 1.1, we find the legal and policy framework imposed by higher levels of government. In some countries, this governmental framing will include legal obligations decreed by supranational organizations. For example, local authorities in countries that are members of the European Union (EU) are required to comply with EU laws and regulations, and to take note of EU policy guidance. Individual nation states determine the legal status, fiscal powers, decision-making powers and functions of local authorities within their boundaries.[21]

As mentioned earlier, some societies put a high value on local democracy and, as we shall see, this gives them a significant advantage. In others, the central state undervalues local government, and overloads itself with functions that it cannot possibly perform well. The good news is that local/central relationships within a given country are subject to negotiation and renegotiation over time.

Why place matters

At 8 pm on Thursday, 26 March 2020, large numbers of people in Britain came to their front doors and windows to applaud the thousands of people who were continuing to go to work and serve the public interest. The UK lockdown had been introduced a few days earlier and, following the example of citizens in Italy, Spain, the Netherlands and other countries, people wanted to give public thanks to those who were keeping society going. Known as 'Clap for carers', a civic moment that took place every Thursday evening for ten weeks, the idea was to thank not just those working in health and social care, but also firefighters, delivery drivers, shop workers, waste collectors, cleaners, postal workers, manufacturers, and so on – in other words, all the essential workers in society.

The threat to society posed by COVID-19 has been met by a strong upsurge in public goodwill. In particular, the virus has spurred a remarkable rise in the number of informal, mutual aid organizations working at very local, or community, level to meet specific needs. COVID-19 has prompted a truly massive increase in volunteering and caring in societies across the world. Some estimates suggested that in the UK, in late March and early April, more than one million people volunteered to help in one way or another – a scale of volunteering not seen in Britain since the Second World War. The point I wish to emphasize here is that *this upswing in social solidarity is almost wholly place-based*. It results from caring individuals living in particular places offering a hand to needy people who live, relatively speaking, very nearby or not too far away.[22]

To claim that place matters could seem to be an odd, even out-of-touch, way of viewing the modern world. Some may feel that, because the internet and mobile phone technologies have transformed our ability to communicate across space – not to mention the way globalization has altered economic and social relations across the entire planet – talking about the importance of place is rather backward looking, even anachronistic. They would be wrong. It is my contention that much of life remains, and will always remain, stubbornly place-dependent.

In this book, I will suggest that place is seriously neglected in modern, national policy making in many countries. It would, however, be misleading to claim that nobody cares much about the quality of place these days. Indeed, the art of place making has been central to the practice of city planning, urban design and architecture for centuries. The good news is that modern practice in place making adopts a multidisciplinary approach and the quality of place-based social, economic and environmental analysis has improved markedly in recent years.[23] The literature on the meaning of place, the impact of place on life chances, the psychology of place-based attachments and the potential political power of place-based feelings of belonging and loyalty is both intriguing and helpful.[24] Here, by drawing on the practice of urbanism as well as the literature on place, I identify three important reasons why place matters to the development of our post COVID-19 strategies.

First, place forms an important part of our identity as human beings. To argue for recognizing the significance of place for our psychological wellbeing is not to contest the value of connections made digitally across space. However, our physical relationships with family, friends, neighbours and colleagues in the area, or city, where we live are vital, because they form part of our identity and help to give meaning to our lives. *Where* we are defines, to some extent, *who* we are.

Daniel Bell and Avner de-Shalit, in a comparative study of cities in eight different countries, explore this theme and show how places express a distinctive ethos or set of values. In a stand against the way globalization is 'flattening cultures', they set out a strong case for recognizing the value of place to our psychological wellbeing:

> ... many people do want to experience particularity, to maintain and nurture their own cultures, values, and

customs that they believe are constitutive of their identities, and without which their communal way of life would be substantially diminished.[25]

Second, if central governments recognize and take advantage of the power of place, they can enhance governmental effectiveness. It is self-evident that places are different. It follows that, if public policy can be tuned more sensitively to the different needs of different areas, then governmental responsiveness can be improved. The background to this argument is that national politicians tend to 'see like a state' rather than 'see like a city'. James Scott shows how, plagued by top-down thinking and the disabling consequences of departmentalism, national governments tend to see like a state.[26] Through various case studies, he shows how central government politicians, and their public servants, often fail to even comprehend the true nature of complex modern challenges and this, inevitably, leads to the development of inappropriate, even disastrous, proposals. Warren Magnusson builds on Scott's analysis and shows how to 'see like a city' or, we might say, to 'see like a place', holds out many benefits.[27] It enables the impact of public policies on communities in a locality to be assessed in the round, and it involves positioning ourselves as inhabitants, not as governors.

Third, place provides the spatial units for the exercise of democracy. The longstanding and fundamental arguments in favour of local government are highly relevant in this context.[28] Developed in varying ways, over a period of more than 150 years, numerous arrangements for organizing local government have emerged across the world. While the institutional design varies, we can say that all general local governments strive to support democratic, place-based policy making. In addition, elected local authorities provide the democratic building blocks that underpin nation states and, ultimately, international democratic institutions.

These, then, are three of the most important reasons why place matters in modern societies. Place forms part of our identity, is critical to governmental effectiveness and underpins democracy.[29] We will return to the theme of place in due course, not least because I will suggest that enhancing the power of place needs to be central to any sound strategy for recovery from the pandemic.

Understanding modern leadership

I have already suggested that good place-based leadership can help societies to recover from the COVID-19 pandemic. But what is leadership? Unfortunately, misconceptions about leadership abound. Worse than that, the national leadership of some countries is, at this point in time, rather dismal. The failings of several incompetent national leaders have been on display at regular COVID-19 televised press conferences and briefings in different countries. The faltering and inadequate response to the emergency of some of these leaders – US President Donald Trump provides a classic example – may even have the unfortunate effect of putting some people off the very idea of leadership. This is to throw the baby out with the bath water – there are very different ways of leading.

As a starting point we can, perhaps, agree that the talents of individual leaders vary enormously. Take a simple example. Jacinda Ardern, Prime Minister of New Zealand since 2017, has shown herself to be an inspirational public leader. Her empathetic style and her outstanding communication skills, on display in many interviews and press conferences, have made a significant difference to the way New Zealand has responded to the COVID-19 challenge. In particular, her decision to take bold measures to restrict the spread of the disease very early on has meant that, on 1 July 2020, COVID-19 had killed 22 people in New Zealand. The contrast between her inclusive approach to leadership and the autocratic style of leadership practised by President Donald Trump could hardly be more striking. The US has the misfortune to be led by a narcissistic bigot, who has a deep disregard for evidence as well as no interest in collaborative decision making. His mishandling of the federal government's response to the US public health emergency has been grotesque. On 1 July 2020, COVID-19 had killed 130,123 people in the US and, as this book goes to press, this figure is rising rather quickly.

However, comparing individual leaders provides only a starting point for a discussion of leadership. Yes, some leaders are good and some are awful. But we need to get behind the performance of particular individuals to ascertain what good public leadership at international, national and local levels actually looks like. What exactly do we mean by leadership? And, in particular, what kinds of public leadership do we need, in order to deal with the COVID-19 challenge?

Let's accept immediately that there is no agreed definition of what 'leadership' means and, indeed, understandings of leadership have shifted over time and remain contested.[30] This does not mean, however, that leadership does not exist or that it doesn't matter. Rather, the contested nature of the term implies a need for discussions of leadership to be sensitive to the context in which it is exercised, to the nature of the leadership task under consideration and to the moral purpose of leadership in that particular context.

While it is an oversimplification, we can caricature two contrasting ways of thinking about leadership. A long-established view of leadership, one that still prevails in much public discourse, is that leadership is a top-down process, one in which senior people 'at the top' issue instructions and/or guidance to their subordinates. This perspective on leadership is, at root, built around the claim that: 'A leader is someone who has followers'. This conceptualization tends to picture leaders as heroic figures, often with charismatic personalities, who have a vision and are well placed to tell their followers what to do.[31]

We can contrast this traditional top-down view of leadership with one that some describe as 'facilitative leadership' and others refer to as 'adaptive leadership'.[32] A facilitative, or adaptive, approach to leadership emphasizes the importance of leaders listening to diverse views and putting significant effort into coalition building. This is not a top-down view of leadership. It resonates with work on 'living' leadership:

> Leadership is not, then about knowing the answers and inspiring others to follow. It is the capacity to release the collective intelligence and insights of groups and organisations. It is helping people to find their own answers.[33]

Two risks arise with this juxtaposition of two contrasting perspectives on the nature and meaning of leadership. First, it simplifies too much. Second, it might be read as implying that leadership emphasizing top-down command and control is, somehow, always suspect, whereas facilitative or adaptive leadership is, on the whole, rather good. This is not my intention. The point I wish to highlight is that leadership style needs to be context-sensitive and task-sensitive. For example, in an extreme emergency – imagine a team of firefighters arriving at a house that is ablaze – it is essential for leaders in positions of authority to take swift decisions on the basis of limited information and to exercise firm command and control. However, most modern public leadership is provided in situations that are not extreme emergencies. It follows that top-down approaches to leadership should be used sparingly.

Taking account of these various debates, and my experience of working with community leaders and city leaders in a number of different countries, I offer my own definition of leadership: 'Leadership is shaping emotions and behaviour to achieve common goals'.[34] Possible strengths of this definition are that it draws attention to how people feel, and it emphasizes the collective construction of common purpose. It prizes respect for the feelings and attitudes of others as well as a strong commitment to collaboration. If exercised wisely, it is imaginative, values risk-taking and involves 'being able to put yourself in the situation of someone else'.[35] We will return to leadership themes in Chapter Four, where I present my New Civic Leadership framework.

Learning from previous disasters

Lucy Jones, a seismologist with the US Geological Survey for over thirty years, has written an intriguing book on natural disasters.[36] In *The Big Ones*, she explains how such disasters have plagued humanity throughout our existence, and she offers an incisive analysis of some of the most famous disruptive natural events that have taken place in world history. She starts out with a description of how the eruption of Mount Vesuvius devastated the Roman City of Pompeii in AD 79 and, eleven world disasters later, concludes with an account of her recent work in Los Angeles aimed at helping the city to prepare for a future earthquake. Her focus is on seismic disruptions and their effects, including tidal waves, floods and so on, not pandemics as such. But her work is a significant contribution to the broader disaster studies literature and it provides many insights for post COVID-19 policy making. In a particularly illuminating final chapter, Jones explains how, towards the end of her career, she spent a year seconded to the City of Los Angeles Mayor's Office, to help with the preparation of a new seismic safety strategy for the city. Her account of this experience provides helpful insights for our discussion of place-based leadership.

Jones argues that 'taking action, taking control' is the best antidote to fear. Interestingly, she explains how many of the most important actions that a community can take happen in local government. She also indicates that a selfish society is a weaker society:

A community whose people know and care about one another is the one that will pull through. A community divided, whose ideas of preparedness involve procuring guns or fortified bunkers, is at risk. It becomes a self-fulfilling prophecy: if you treat your neighbour as a potential enemy, you make him one, and in so doing contribute to your society's collapse.[37]

In a key passage, Jones stresses that it is important to recognize that disasters are *more than the moment at which they happen*. She argues that, to manage disasters effectively, leaders, communities and individuals must focus on three different time periods: 1) prepare before any given event, in order to minimize damage and adverse impacts; 2) respond effectively during the event to save lives; and 3) bring people together as a community after the event to rebuild and recover. She emphasizes that it is important to expand our definition of preparedness beyond simply thinking about how to respond. Efforts made before *and after* the event are vital for societal recovery.

The literature on how to create resilient cities and localities, which has grown rapidly in recent years, is relevant in this context. A 2019 report from the Rockefeller Foundation's '100 Resilient Cities' initiative provides some helpful suggestions.[38] A related approach to creating resilient societies is the Build Back Better (BBB) method developed by various international organizations.[39] This is an approach to post-disaster recovery that reduces vulnerability to future disasters, and builds community resilience to address future physical, social, environmental and economic shocks.

Three main insights from the disaster recovery and resilient cities literature are particularly important for post COVID-19 strategy. First, having good local governance matters a great deal. Crisis interventions and rescue missions will always hit the headlines when disaster strikes. The inspiring stories of immediate responses by state and non-state actors to human suffering are to be applauded. But, unsung in media accounts, it is having tolerably good local governance arrangements in place – before, during and after a disaster – that saves lives and underpins societal recovery.

Second, good place-based leaders can make a huge difference. Yes, wise national leadership and international leadership are needed when a pandemic, or similar disaster, impacts a country or countries. But it is important to recognize that local leaders are rooted in their communities – they are close to the ground, they can access local knowledge and resources and, if they are empathetic leaders, they can make an emotional connection that can, in turn, stimulate all kinds of invaluable collective action.

Third, cities and localities that look ahead, develop a farsighted vision for their area, and have firm strategic plans in place for delivering that vision are far better placed to respond to a crisis. Having a vision, preferably a well-known vision that enjoys public support, enables leaders to move swiftly from being reactive to being proactive, even as disaster strikes. This is because the city, or locality, has developed a solid understanding of the future it wants for its people.

Conclusions

This chapter has opened up some new ways of thinking about what the COVID-19 threat might mean for modern societies. Vast numbers of people have died, even larger numbers have been infected. Millions have lost their jobs and poor people have suffered a lot more than the better off. Those of us who have been living in countries that have had lockdowns imposed upon us have had our lives disrupted as never before. This is not a complaint, more an attempt to comprehend that the nature of the challenges we are now all having to deal with will require a response that is transformative. There will be those who will disagree. They will say, 'No, no – this is, admittedly, a bit of a setback, but the sooner we get back to the society we had in 2019 the better'.

I have titled this chapter 'No Going Back' for a reason. Yes, most of us want a return to some kind of normality, in the sense of being able to leave our homes as and when we wish.

How good it would be to be able to go out and engage in social and other activities that we value and find fulfilling. Better still to have a satisfying job and a secure future. But COVID-19 imposes a more demanding set of questions that we cannot avoid. It raises issues about governance that are just as profound as health, poverty and economic prosperity. Stated bluntly, without good governance it is not possible to protect public health, to tackle poverty and to deliver prosperity. Why has this dreadful pandemic happened? What does it reveal about the nature of the societies we have created in recent decades? What do we need to do to upgrade our systems of governance, so that we are better able to anticipate and respond to future threats?

This book does not claim to provide ready answers to these questions. Wise answers can only stem from widespread conversations and dialogue – from collective exchange and social discovery in communities, localities and cities across the world. The argument that will be presented in the following pages is, however, a thoroughly hopeful one. If we recognize that there is 'no going back', the future holds out the exciting prospect of developing new ways of co-creating prosperous and just societies that respect and value the natural world on which we all depend.

Notes

[1]   The figures relating to COVID-19 presented in this book relate to 1 July 2020 unless stated otherwise.

[2]   The Spanish Flu of 2018 infected around 500 million people and killed 50–100 million. See Spinney L. (2018) *Pale Rider: The Spanish flu of 1918 and how it changed the world*, Vintage: London.

[3]   The precise origins of the 'Think globally, act locally' slogan are contested. Friends of the Earth, founded in 1971, certainly extolled this strategy in the early 1970s.

[4]   For example, movements like Extinction Rebellion, founded in 2018, are becoming increasingly influential: https://rebellion.earth. See also: Thunberg G. (2019) *No One is Too Small to Make a Difference*, London: Penguin.

[5] This is the central theme of my recent book: Hambleton R. (2015) *Leading the Inclusive City: Place-based innovation for a bounded planet*, Bristol: Policy Press.

[6] Giordano P. (2020) *How Contagion Works: Science, awareness and community in times of global crises*, London: Weidenfeld and Nicolson, p 39.

[7] Giordano (2020) (see Note 6), p 26.

[8] Jones T. (2020) 'The rebirth of humanity', *The Observer*, 12 April, p 14.

[9] Tooze A. (2020) 'COVID-19 means that it's not the economy any more, stupid', *The Guardian*, 21 March.

[10] The idea of promoting societal wellbeing rather than 'economic growth' per se is not a new one. For example, two influential organizations were founded in 1986: The New Economics Foundation (https://neweconomics.org) and the Centre for Local Economic Strategies (https://cles.org.uk). Also, the UK Office for National Statistics now publishes statistics on wellbeing, although these are not given sufficient attention in public policy debates: https://www.ons.gov.uk/peoplepopulationandcommunity/wellbeing

[11] See, for example: Stiglitz J.E. (1989) *The Economic Role of the State*, Oxford: Blackwell; Stiglitz J.E. (2004) *The Roaring Nineties*, London: Penguin; Stiglitz J.E. (2006) *Making Globalization Work*, London: Allen Lane; and Stiglitz J.E. (2020) *People, Power and Profits: Progressive capitalism for an age of discontent*, London: Penguin.

[12] In recent years, other scholars have built on the analysis presented by Stiglitz. See, for example: Raworth K. (2017) *Doughnut Economics: Seven ways to think like a 21st century economist*, London: Random House Business; and Mazzucato M. (2019) *The Value of Everything: Making and taking in the global economy*, London: Penguin.

[13] Sandel M.J. (2012) *What Money Can't Buy: The moral limits of markets*, London: Allen Lane, p 7.

[14] See Hambleton (2015, pp 6–9) (Note 5).

[15] See, for example, Mason P. (2015) *Post Capitalism: A guide to our future*, London: Penguin Books; and Monbiot G. (2017) *Out of the Wreckage: A new politics for an age of crisis*, London: Verso.

[16] See, for example: Girardet H. (2008) *Cities, People, Planet: Urban development and climate change* (2nd edn), Chichester: John Wiley; Jackson T. (2009) *Prosperity Without Growth: Economics for a finite planet*, London: Earthscan; and Bulkeley H. (2013) *Cities and Climate Change*, Abingdon: Routledge.

[17] Brenner N., Marcuse P. and Mayer M. (2012) *Cities for People, Not for Profit: Critical urban theory and the right to the city*, Abingdon: Routledge. See also: Lefebvre H. (1967) 'The right to the city', in E. Kofman and E. Lebas (eds) (1996) *Writings on Cities*, Blackwell: London.

[18] Hirschman A.O. (1970) *Exit, Voice and Loyalty*, Cambridge, MA: Harvard University Press.

[19] Peterson P.E. (1981) *City Limits*, Chicago, IL: University of Chicago Press.

[20] See, for example, Savitch H.V. and Kantor P. (2002) *Cities in the International Marketplace: The political economy of urban development in North America and Western Europe*, Princeton, NJ: Princeton University Press.

[21] In countries with a federal system of government, the federal government usually devolves decisions about the status, power and functions of local governments to the state level. See, for example, the US and Canada.

[22] It is worth celebrating the various 'Friendly Neighbours' initiatives that have sprung up. These community-based efforts involve a neighbourhood creating funds and resources for *other* less well-off neighbourhoods.

[23] See, for example: Shaftoe H. (2008) *Convivial Urban Spaces: Creating effective public places*, London: Earthscan; Gehl J. (2010) *Cities for People*, Washington, DC: Island Press; and Barton H. (2017) *City of Wellbeing: A radical guide to planning*, London: Routledge. There are also many organizations campaigning to improve the quality of places, including the Royal Town Planning Institute (https://www.rtpi.org.uk) and the Place Alliance (http://placealliance.org.uk).

[24] Useful starting points for the interested reader are: Tuan Y.F. (1977) *Space and Place: The perspective of experience*, Minneapolis, MN: The University of Minneapolis Press; De Blij H. (2009) *The Power of Place: Geography, destiny and globalization's rough landscape*, Oxford: Oxford University Press; Castello L. (2010) *Rethinking the Meaning of Place: Conceiving place in architecture-urbanism*, Farnham: Ashgate; and McClay W.M. and McAllister T.V. (eds) (2014) *Why Place Matters: Geography, identity and civic life in modern America*, New York, NY: Encounter Books.

[25] Bell D.A. and de-Shalit A. (2011) *The Spirit of Cities. Why the identity of a city matters in a global age*, Princeton, NJ: University of Princeton Press, p 5.

[26] Scott J. (1998) *Seeing Like a State: How certain schemes to improve the human condition have failed*, Newhaven, CT: Yale University Press.

[27] Magnusson W. (2011) *Politics of Urbanism: Seeing like a city*, Abingdon: Routledge.

[28] United Cities and Local Governments (2009) *Decentralisation and Local Democracy in the World 2008*, Barcelona: United Cities and Local Governments; Loughlin J., Hendriks F. and Lidstrom A. (eds) (2012) *The Oxford Handbook of Local and Regional Democracy in Europe*, Oxford: Oxford University Press.

[29] The case for paying more attention to place in public policy and management is set out in more detail in: Hambleton (2015, pp 80–97) (see Note 5).

[30] There is an extensive literature on leadership. Books I recommend are: Grint K. (2005) *Leadership: Limits and possibilities*, Basingstoke: Palgrave; Keohane N.O. (2010) *Thinking about Leadership*, Princeton, NJ: Princeton University Press; and Bolden R., Witzel M. and Linacre N. (eds) (2016) *Leadership Paradoxes: Rethinking leadership for an uncertain world*, London: Routledge.

[31] See, for example, Adair J. (2002) *Inspiring Leadership: Learning from great leaders*, London: Thorogood Publishing.

[32] Svara J.H. (1998) *Facilitative Leadership in Local Government: Lessons from successful mayors and chairpersons*, San Francisco, CA: Jossey-Bass; Heifetz R., Grashow A. and Linsky M. (2009) *The Practice of Adaptive Leadership*, Boston, MA: Harvard Business School.

[33] Binney G., Wilke G. and Williams C. (2012) *Living Leadership: A practical guide for ordinary heroes*, Harlow: Pearson Education.

[34] Hambleton R. (2007) 'New leadership for democratic urban space' in R. Hambleton and J.S. Gross (eds) *Governing Cities in a Global Era: Urban innovation, competition and democratic reform*, Basingstoke: Palgrave, p 174.

[35] Keohane N.O. (2010) *Thinking About Leadership*, Princeton, NJ: Princeton University Press, p 89.

[36] Jones L. (2018) *The Big Ones: How natural disasters have shaped humanity*, London: Icon Books Ltd.

[37] See Jones (2018, p 226) (see Note 36).

[38] Rockefeller Foundation (2019) *Resilient Cities. Resilient Lives: Lessons from the 100 resilient cities network*, New York, NY: Rockefeller Foundation. See also: Pearson L.J., Newton P.W. and Roberts P. (eds) (2014) *Resilient Sustainable Cities: A future*, London: Routledge.

[39] See, for example, the work of the United Nations Office for Disaster Risk Reduction: https://www.unisdr.org/files/53213_bbb.pdf

TWO

The COVID-19 Pandemic

Introduction

This chapter provides a concise overview of the COVID-19 pandemic. By drawing on the extensive news output and published scientific reports, the aim is to explain what a coronavirus is, to identify the origins of the COVID-19 pandemic, and to provide an international overview of the way the disease spread so rapidly across the world. Attention then turns to consider the performance of UK central government. A final section considers the main features of the COVID-19 pandemic, and identifies some of the key policy issues that the disease now presents to societies across the world.

What is a coronavirus?

First discovered in domesticated chickens in the 1930s, coronaviruses are a group of viruses that cause disease in animals. Seven, including COVID-19, have made the jump from animals to humans. When first discovered in humans in the 1960s, the viruses were found to cause relatively mild, cold-like symptoms. However, more lethal versions have emerged in more recent years.

Severe acute respiratory syndrome (SARS), the first deadly epidemic caused by a coronavirus, reached 29 countries in 2002 and 2003. Infecting around 8,000 people, and killing just over 800, it was contained by good public policy coupled with an element of good fortune. Traditional public health measures, such as testing, isolating patients and screening people at airports and elsewhere, proved to be effective. However, SARS was easier to control than COVID-19, because it was less transmissible; those infected were probably not contagious until they were very ill.

First reported in Saudi Arabia, another lethal coronavirus is Middle East respiratory syndrome (MERS). Emerging in 2012, this virus appears to be particularly deadly for those who catch it. At the end of 2019, 2,494 cases had been recorded and 34% of those infected – 858 people – had died. However, it seems that this virus does not pass that easily from person to person, and most infections have arisen in hospital or other healthcare settings.

The main COVID-19 symptoms are similar to other coronaviruses: fever, cough and shortness of breath.[1] However, COVID-19 differs in three significant ways. First, the spectrum of the disease is much wider, with many of those affected experiencing a relatively mild infection. Indeed, it is likely that many people are carrying the disease without displaying any symptoms at all, and this makes it harder to control. Second, while around 80 per cent of those affected are likely to have a mild infection, some 20 per cent are likely to experience a severe illness. The death rate varies between 1.7 per cent and 3.4 per cent, with a key factor being access to high-quality hospital care. In developing countries, with under-resourced healthcare systems, the death rate is much higher than in developed countries. Third, the COVID-19 pandemic is truly seismic in scale and impact. On 1 July 2020, there were 10.6 million confirmed cases and 514,000 people had died.

The emergence of the COVID-19 pandemic

It is almost certainly the case that the COVID-19 virus emerged from the Huanan wet market in Wuhan, the capital city of central China's Hubei province, in December 2019.[2] While public records on the early incidence of this new virus are scant, we know that some vendors who worked at the wet market – where dead and live animals are traded – became ill in December 2019, possibly earlier. On 30 December 2019, Li Wenliang, an ophthalmologist working at Wuhan central hospital, shared a message with some of his friends in a WeChat group, indicating that he thought seven people in the hospital had contracted SARS, and warned them to be careful. He wasn't to know at the time that the illness he referred to was not SARS, but a new virus, which was later to be named COVID-19.

The Chinese government has been criticized for not sharing information about the appearance of this new virus at an early stage. Indeed, on 3 January 2020, Li Wenliang was visited by the Wuhan police and admonished for spreading false rumours.[3] A subsequent inquiry exonerated him, and the Chinese Communist Party offered a 'solemn apology'. Li Wenliang continued to work at the hospital and, in a tragic turn of events, he contracted COVID-19 and died on 7 February 2020. The 33-year-old is now widely recognized as a remarkably brave and principled public servant.

On 31 December 2019, China alerted the World Health Organization (WHO) to the fact that it had identified 34 cases of pneumonia stemming from an unknown virus. This was, then, the date when the world at large was made aware of this mysterious disease. The Chinese authorities closed down the Huanan wet market the following day, and within a week they had isolated a virus, which was subsequently identified as a new type of coronavirus.

Where did the virus causing the COVID-19 pandemic come from? Laura Spinney, a British science journalist, explains that the virus is the product of natural evolution.[4] She notes that a study of its genetic sequence by Scripps Research (formerly known as the Scripps Research Institute) in California rules out the possibility that it could have been manufactured in a lab. It seems likely that the original reservoir for the virus was bats. Exactly how the virus spread from bats to people is uncertain. However, Spinney suggests, and others agree with her, that it is likely that the virus was transmitted from bats to humans via an intermediate animal host, possibly a pangolin. This leads some to blame the Chinese cultural practice of eating pangolins, regarded as a delicacy in some Chinese circles, for the pandemic.

But, this is only part of the story. As revealed in a study of factory farming by Rob Wallace, an evolutionary biologist, the density with which chickens, turkeys and other poultry are packed together in massive hangars ratchets up the virulence of a virus and makes it far more dangerous.[5] Spinney explains how, starting in the 1990s, as part of its economic transformation, China ramped up food production systems to an industrial scale. A consequence was that smallholding farmers were pushed out of the livestock industry. Searching for a new way of generating an income, some of them turned to farming wild species that had previously been eaten for subsistence only.[6] Spinney concludes that it is clear that China's wet markets will need to be much better regulated, but she also shows how we need to engage in a major rethink in how our food is produced globally. Clearly, local food production needs to be given a major boost.

It is important to understand that China's massive poultry industry is not wholly Chinese-owned. For example, Goldman Sachs, the New York–based investment bank, has substantial holdings in the industry. Thus, powerful place-less actors, to use the phrase I introduced in Chapter One, played a key role in promoting the conditions that led to the COVID-19 pandemic.

Mark Honigsbaum, a medical historian and journalist, provides solid evidence to back this interpretation. His book, *The Pandemic Century*, explains how human exploitation of the planet has, repeatedly, disturbed the ecological equilibriums in which pathogens habitually reside, and that these disruptions have then caused diseases.[7] This, he suggests, is particularly true for animal origin, or zoonotic, diseases like COVID-19.

We can already see, then, that efforts to prevent future pandemics can be closely aligned with steps to address climate change. For example, reducing food miles – meaning the distance that food is transported from the place of its making to the consumer – addresses both global warming and public health challenges. Factory farming exploits animals, by cramming them together in an intolerable way in order to boost profits. Around two thirds of farm animals in the world are factory farmed each year, that is nearly 50 billion animals. People who care about animal welfare, public health and global warming are clear that this practice needs to be stopped. It goes without saying that, as vegetarians and vegans are entitled to point out, if we did not eat meat, we would make a massive contribution to tackling global warming and, in addition, there would have been no COVID-19 pandemic.[8]

The global spread of COVID-19

It is not very easy to access reliable data on either the growth in the number of COVID-19 cases or the number of people dying from COVID-19. This is partly because different countries may have decided to manipulate or under-report the figures, and partly because record keeping in just about all countries faces difficult challenges.

For example, in the UK context it was widely recognized in April 2020 that the number of new COVID-19 cases being reported each day by the government was almost certainly a poor reflection of the actual number of people who had been infected. At that time, the figures for new deaths reported in daily announcements by central government only included deaths in hospital of patients who had tested positive for coronavirus. Deaths caused by COVID-19 in care homes, or other locations outside hospitals, were not included. It follows that the official UK figures announced at daily press briefings in April understated the actual death rate to a remarkable degree.

Accepting necessary caveats about the limitations of the data, we can say that the COVID-19 virus spread fairly quickly within China. On 22 January 2020, the government reported 571 confirmed cases and 17 deaths. The following day, China imposed a draconian lockdown in Wuhan and other cities in Hubei in an effort to block the spread of the disease. Highly restrictive lockdowns were soon imposed in cities and provinces across China. The evidence suggests that this forthright action had the effect of limiting the spread of COVID-19. The death rate in China soared, but appeared to level out after a few weeks. On 19 March, China reported no new cases for the first time since the pandemic began and on, 7 April, China reported no new deaths.

On 30 January 2020, the WHO declared 'a public health emergency of international concern'[9] and, three days later, the first death outside China was recorded in the Philippines. On 11 February, the WHO announced that the name of this new virus was COVID-19. This name is a shortened version of corona (Co) virus (vi) disease (d), with 19 referring to 2019, the year the virus first appeared.

In the next few weeks, the disease spread very rapidly indeed to a large number of countries. On 11 March, Dr Tedros Adhanom Ghebreyesus, Director-General of the WHO, indicated that there were then 118,000 COVID-19 cases in 114 countries, and that 4,291 people had lost their lives. He indicated that he was deeply concerned both by the alarming levels of spread and severity, and by the alarming levels of inaction. He announced that COVID-19 should now be considered a pandemic, defined as the 'global spread of a new disease'. He pointed out that this was the first pandemic caused by a coronavirus, and that it was also the first pandemic that could be controlled. He urged governments to be far more proactive in responding to the threat:

'WHO has been in full response mode since we were notified of the first cases. And we have called every day for countries to take urgent and aggressive action. We have rung the alarm bell loud and clear … We cannot say this loudly enough, or clearly enough, or often enough: all countries can still change the course of this pandemic. If countries detect, test, treat, isolate, trace, and mobilise their people in response, those with a handful of cases can prevent those cases becoming clusters, and those clusters becoming community transmission.'[10]

In a video posted on the WHO website on 16 March, Dr Ghebreyesus could hardly contain his frustration at the lack of urgency he was encountering in some countries: 'You cannot fight a fire blindfolded … We have a simple message for all countries: test, test, test.'[11]

The responses of national governments have varied. Several Asian countries, perhaps because they had learned painful lessons from their experiences with SARS and MERS, acted quickly and decisively to introduce robust testing and containment strategies. It seems likely that the distress caused by the earlier outbreaks spurred on officials to be more aggressive in tackling COVID-19, and possibly made residents more willing to accept the relatively intrusive steps that were being taken to locate and contain the disease. For example, South Korea developed testing for the virus even before it had a significant number of cases. They have used testing aggressively to identify cases, not only testing people who are so sick that they have to be admitted to hospital, but also mild cases and even suspected cases. Hong Kong and Singapore have pursued similar strategies in responding to the outbreak. This emphasis on testing, isolating and tracing was successful in flattening the rising curve in the growth in the numbers of COVID-19 cases and deaths in these countries.

In closing this discussion of the global spread of the disease, I offer a graph of the rise in global deaths from COVID-19 and

Figure 2.1: Global deaths from COVID-19

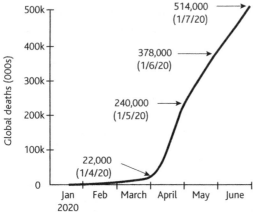

Source: Worldmeter: https://worldmeters.info/coronavirus/

some figures relating to particular countries. It is upsetting to have to record that, by the time you see these appalling figures, they will be even worse than indicated here. A useful source of information on the latest COVID-19 figures is provided by the Worldometer service.[12] Figure 2.1 shows the vertiginous rise in the global number of deaths from COVID-19 up to the end of June 2020. In January 2020, fewer than 1,000 had died; by the end of June 2020, the figure was over 500,000. For comparison, we can note that, for example, the number of British civilians who died in the Second World War was 70,000 and the total number of US deaths in the Vietnam War was 58,000.

Table 2.1 shows the five countries with the highest number of COVID-19 deaths as recorded on 1 July 2020. Table 2.2 shows five countries with a relatively low number of COVID-19 deaths, also as recorded on 1 July 2020. It is obvious that countries with relatively large populations might be expected to have larger numbers of cases and deaths. This factor can be removed by comparing the total number of COVID-19 cases and deaths per million

Table 2.1: Countries with the highest number of COVID-19 deaths

Country	Total cases	Total deaths	Total cases per million pop.	Total deaths per million pop.
1) US	2,727,996	130,123	8,242	393
2) Brazil	1,408,485	59,656	6,626	281
3) UK	312,654	43,730	4,606	644
4) India	585,792	17,410	424	13
5) Russia	654,405	9,536	4,484	65

Note: The figures in this table relate to 1 July 2020.
Source: Worldometer: https://www.worldometers.info/coronavirus/

population. If we look at the number of deaths per million people, we can see that New Zealand (four deaths) has, so far, been around 161 times more effective in preventing deaths from COVID-19 than the UK (644 deaths).

The performance of UK national government

It is too early to provide an exhaustive evaluation of the strengths and weaknesses of the strategy adopted by the UK Conservative government, but the signs are not promising.[13] Table 2.1 suggests that the UK performs very badly when compared with the other countries listed in Table 2.2.

A judge-led independent public inquiry will be needed in the coming period, to gather evidence from key actors, operating inside and outside the state, to understand what happened and where responsibility lies. Key tasks for this inquiry will be: to establish what happened and when; to identify who decided what actions to take and why; to share the evidence base under-pinning these various decisions; to assess the distributional impact of these decisions on different groups and communities within the UK; and to learn specific lessons for future policy and practice. A process of open and self-critical examination of what transpired will be enormously important in establishing

Table 2.2: Countries with relatively low numbers of COVID-19 deaths (selected)

Country	Total cases	Total deaths	Total cases per million pop.	Total deaths per million pop.
1) Hong Kong	1,206	7	161	0.9
2) New Zealand	1,528	22	305	4.0
3) Singapore	44,122	26	7,542	4.0
4) Australia	7,920	104	311	4.0
5) South Korea	12,768	605	251	6.0

Note: The figures in this table relate to 1 July 2020.
Source: Worldometer: https://www.worldometers.info/coronavirus/

future public confidence in government – a theme to which we will return in Chapter Three. It follows that these inquiries will need to be well resourced and thorough.

However, in advance of those inquiries, it is already possible to identify a number of concerns that future investigations will surely wish to examine. It is helpful to divide a discussion of UK government performance into two episodes: the pre-COVID-19 period; and the response to COVID-19.

The pre-COVID-19 period: was the UK prepared?

It is important to go back to November 2019, before the first murmurings of a strange new virus were starting to emerge from Wuhan, China, and to ask probing questions about the state of readiness of British public services. The spending figures show that UK public services had suffered extensive cuts in funding in the period since 2010 due to central government policies pursued in the name of so-called 'austerity'. For example, National Health Service (NHS) budgets rose by only 1.5 per cent a year in the ten years between 2009–10 and 2018–19, compared with the 3.7 per cent average since the NHS was established. A direct consequence was that the health service could not possibly keep pace with the growing healthcare needs of a population that was both growing and aging – a population that was also experiencing increasing levels of obesity and diabetes.

Meanwhile, in the same decade, the financial support to local government, which provides vital services for some of the most vulnerable in society, was decimated. For example, a National Audit Office study carried out in 2018 showed that, between 2010–11 and 2017–18, local authority spending on social care in England fell by 49 per cent in real terms.[14] Another 2018 study, this one carried out by the Local Government Association, showed that local authorities in England had suffered a cut of nearly £16 billion in their level of core funding from central government in the period since 2010.[15] This meant that councils lost 60p out of every £1 the government had previously provided. Inevitably, many local authority services simply had to be withdrawn.

A good indicator of extreme poverty is provided by the provision of emergency food aid to people in desperate need. The figures show that, in the period from 2010, there has been an astonishing foodbank explosion in the UK. The Trussel Trust, which accounts for about two thirds of all foodbanks in the country, provided 41,000 food parcels in 2009–10; in 2018–19, the figure was 1.6 million.[16] Recent analysis of expenditure patterns shows that Labour councils have borne the brunt of the local government cuts imposed by central government in the last decade. On average, Labour councils saw their spending power reduced by 34 per cent, while the average Conservative council received a cut of 24 per cent.[17]

In October 2016, the government carried out a simulation exercise to assess the likely impact of a hypothetical influenza pandemic on the UK. The simulation, known as Exercise Cygnus, showed that the health system would be in very deep trouble, because it lacked the necessary resources. The report, which was sent to all major government departments in July

2017, predicted a shortage of hospital beds, medical equipment, morgue capacity and personal protective equipment (PPE). The government ignored the evidence and took no action. In April 2020, the government refused a freedom of information request by *The Guardian* to publish the report. This effort to suppress important evidence proved futile, as the report was leaked to *The Guardian* on 7 May 2020.[18]

An in-depth analysis of UK public policy in the 2010–20 period notes that real wages, adjusted for inflation, dropped by 5 per cent, that work became increasingly precarious and that the whole tone of public life was coarsened.[19] In line with Thatcherism, the government's overall approach was designed to reduce the size of the state and to promote self-interested individualism. Interestingly, the Conservative Party adopted a rather different policy offer when campaigning ahead of the General Election held in December 2019. The simplistic slogan used by the Conservative Party in the election was 'Get Brexit Done' but, to the surprise of many, Prime Minister Johnson also promised significant increases in public spending:

> 'Here was a covert admission that austerity had not only been deeply damaging, but unnecessary, a mere expedient, a prolonged exercise in what they could get away with in pursuit of their core ambition of shrinking the state. Once the polls turned and an election loomed, the Tories dissembled.'[20]

The impact of these major cuts in public spending fell disproportionately on poor people, with the result that social and economic inequality in the country increased significantly. In 2018, Philip Alston, the United Nations Special Rapporteur on extreme poverty and human rights, carried out a study that revealed that 14 million people, a fifth of the population in the UK, were living in poverty. He concluded that the UK's social safety net had been deliberately removed and replaced with a harsh and uncaring ethos.[21]

Worse was to come when, in 2020, a report on health equity by Sir Michael Marmot and colleagues shocked the nation.[22] Sir Michael stated that 'England was faltering' and his report revealed that, in the previous ten years, the health gap between wealthy and deprived areas had grown, that improvements in life expectancy had, after more than a century of improvement, stalled and that, unbelievably, life expectancy for very poor women was actually in decline. In an article summarizing his findings Sir Michael shows how a decade of austerity resulted in a decline in overall health in England and that, because public spending was redirected away from areas of greatest need, health inequalities rose sharply.[23]

The evidence suggests, then, that the government's pursuit of an uncaring 'austerity' agenda for the ten years from 2010 left our public services critically weakened. At the same time, the growth of precarious work, promoted by the government's unwise economic policies, left many people and families extremely vulnerable to economic downturns.[24] It is difficult not to conclude that, in December 2019, the UK was, as a direct consequence of government policy, decidedly unprepared for the COVID-19 onslaught.

How good was the UK government response to COVID-19?

In January 2020, Conservative ministers, fresh from victory in the General Election held on 12 December 2019, were concentrating on delivering on their promise to take Britain out of the European Union by their declared target date of the end of that month. In his New Year's Day message, Prime Minister Johnson promised 'a fantastic year and a remarkable decade for the United Kingdom'. With hindsight it appears that the governmental obsession with Brexit drowned out the messages, already arriving in the UK in mid-January, suggesting that a deeply troubling new disease was spiralling out of control in China. The Prime Minister and his government ignored these troubling signals for several weeks.

Consider the time line. As noted earlier, on 31 January 2020, the WHO declared 'a public health emergency of international concern'. The first death in France from COVID-19 was recorded on 14 February and, on 23 February, Italy noted that it had suffered three fatalities and had started to cancel public events. Large areas of Europe were already being put under lockdown. On 3 March 2020, in an astonishingly crass performance, a smiling Boris Johnson appeared on a nationally televised press conference, one that was specifically designed to draw public attention to the gravity of the COVID-19 emergency, explaining how he was 'shaking hands with everyone', including at a hospital treating coronavirus patients.

On 10–13 March, the Cheltenham Festival, a major English horseracing event, went ahead despite widespread expressions of public concern. Over 250,000 people attended and, inevitably, this very large gathering had the effect of super-spreading the COVID-19 infection. The Jockey Club, owners of the Festival, justified its decision to go ahead with the Festival, by pointing out that Prime Minister Johnson had attended the England versus Wales international rugby match at Twickenham a few days earlier. It was, indeed, true that Boris Johnson had demonstrated his poor understanding of the nature of the public health crisis facing the country by going to the rugby international on 7 March.

Richard Horton, the editor-in-chief of *The Lancet*, one of the world's most respected medical journals, has presented detailed evidence showing that the UK government disregarded the clear warning signs coming from China. He suggests that there was a 'collective failure' to appreciate the enormity of the COVID-19 pandemic and to enact swift measures to protect the public. While he indicated that he had 'utmost respect' for the two advisers who stood alongside Boris Johnson at the unbecoming 3 March press conference – Professor Chris Whitty, the Chief Medical Officer, and Sir Patrick Vallance, the Chief Scientific Adviser – Horton stated: 'Somewhere there has been a collective failure among politicians and perhaps even government experts to recognise the signals that Chinese and Italian scientists were sending'.[25]

Sadly, the official figures on the number of people dying from COVID-19 in the UK in recent months demonstrate that Dr Horton was right. For example, in South Korea (population 52 million) the death toll from COVID-19 on 1 July 2020 was 605. The figure for the UK (population 66 million) on the same date was 43,730. Table 2.1 and Table 2.2 provide more details.

The government's policy, already stumbling and incompetent, took a turn for the worse when it emerged, on 22 May 2020, that Dominic Cummings, Prime Minister Johnson's most senior adviser, had ignored the government's lockdown rules and driven with his wife and son 260 miles from London to Durham. This journey took place on the weekend of 28–29 March, when the country was in lockdown and the official guidance was: 'Stay at home; Protect our NHS; Save lives'. On 22 May, *The Guardian* and the *Daily Mirror* published the story, and Downing Street responded by saying that the journey was 'essential'.

The newspapers persisted with their enquiries and published a follow-up story demonstrating that on Easter Sunday (12 April), his wife's birthday, Cummings had taken a 60-mile round trip from Durham to Barnard Castle, a well-known beauty spot. This led to howls of public protest, outrage and anger. An opinion poll, published on 31 May, showed that 81 per cent of people believed that Cummings had broken the rules, and 68 per cent said he should resign, including 52 per cent of Conservative supporters.[26] Astonishingly, Cummings refused to resign and Johnson refused to sack him. Scientists and health administrators explained that public faith in government is essential in a public health crisis, and that trust had been badly damaged by Cummings, giving the impression that there was one rule for the people and another rule for the elite. They argued that for Cummings to continue in office would undermine the crucial public health messages the government was trying to put across and would cost lives. The Prime Minister ignored them.

The performance of the UK Conservative government has been deplorable and it has, almost certainly, cost tens of thousands of lives. In July, Anthony Costello, a former WHO director, was asked how many deaths the UK government could have prevented and his answer was horrifying:

> 'I honestly think we could have prevented about 50,000 of them, if we'd gone early like South Korea. I think the Scientific Advisory Group for Emergencies (SAGE) got it wrong, Public Health England (PHE) got it wrong, and Boris Johnson got it wrong.'[27]

Opposition parties in the UK parliament are rightly holding government ministers to account for the decisions they have made, and there is certain to be an in-depth public inquiry. Some of the important issues that will surely attract further scrutiny include:

- the claim that, in February and early March 2020, the government's policy was to reduce the impact of the virus, by allowing it to pass through the entire population, so that the country could acquire 'herd immunity';
- the failure of the government to take up several invitations from the European Union to participate in international arrangements to bulk-buy masks, gowns, gloves, ventilators and other necessary equipment for health and care workers;
- the reasons why the government ignored WHO advice to prioritize the successful strategy, deployed in other countries, of testing, treating, tracing and isolating infected people;
- the critical shortages of PPE for people working on the front line, not just in health and social care settings, but also for staff working in other front-line roles, for example in public transport, the fire service and the police service;

- the failure, for several weeks, to record and publish, on a daily basis, the number of deaths in care homes and the community alongside figures on the deaths occurring in hospitals;
- the failure of the Prime Minister to sack Dominic Cummings in May 2020, even though his continued presence in government was undermining the core public health message of the government.

Understanding the challenges set down by COVID-19

The COVID-19 pandemic is shaking up our world in ways that are difficult to comprehend. The sheer scale of the challenge, the startling pace of change, the awful intensity of human suffering, these all throw down an immense gauntlet to society at large and, in particular, to civic leaders at all levels of governance – neighbourhood, local authority, regional, national and international.

The COVID-19 challenge – or, in truth, the multiple challenges of COVID-19 – is truly daunting. But this does not mean that these challenges cannot be addressed. Here I introduce two themes designed to highlight the main issues and tensions that we now face. These will be revisited in later chapters.

The complexity of the COVID-19 challenge

It is almost fifty years since two professors at the University of California, Berkeley co-wrote an article that was to have a major impact not just on planning theory, but also on our understanding of public leadership as well as modern systems thinking. Horst Rittel, a design theorist, and Melvin Webber, a professor of planning, argued, in essence, that there are two kinds of problems facing modern societies.[28] 'Tame' problems may be fiendishly complicated, but they can probably be resolved in a step-by-step fashion because, at root, there is only a limited degree of uncertainty; they are akin to puzzles.[29] A 'wicked' public policy problem is, however, altogether more complex, not least because the relationships between cause and effect are unclear. Moreover, there may be insufficient agreement about the nature of the public good, and various stakeholders in the policy process can be expected to have competing ideas about how to solve the problem.

As my colleague Richard Bolden, a professor of leadership and management, has argued, the COVID-19 pandemic is an inherently complex problem – one that requires multiple domains in society to make sense of the issues and to mobilize timely and effective responses.[30] COVID-19 is, then, a classic example of a 'wicked' problem. Bolden suggests that an effective response will require leaders to lead without formal authority and to use systems thinking to initiate new patterns of behaviour that spread from one context to another. His analysis is perspicacious and we will draw on it later. At this point, it is enough to record that there can be no simple answers to the complexity of the COVID-19 challenge, and there is certainly no 'silver bullet'. More than that, while the deployment of high-quality science will be essential in addressing this challenge, an effective response to COVID-19 goes way beyond science. Effective solutions require the exercise of wise political judgement. Even the very best science cannot deliver the answers. Politicians who advocate simple solutions, and attempt to reduce public policy choices to superficial slogans, would be well advised to consider more carefully the true complexity of the COVID-19 emergency.

COVID-19: some policy issues

Stemming from the complexity of the COVID-19 challenge, just described, there are a number of challenges, but also opportunities, now facing civic leaders as they examine the evidence, develop their own understanding and consider forward strategy. Robert Muggah and Thomas Ermacora provide a helpful checklist of nine topics for attention: 1) places will need to retro-fitted; 2) the shift to online retail can be expected to accelerate; 3) urban mobility will undergo a series of corrections, and space for pedestrians and cyclists will need to be expanded; 4) the way societies produce and consume food will be overhauled; 5) privacy and politics will be deeply affected by the growth of surveillance; 6) there could be a climate dividend; 7) the virus is strengthening social cohesion in some cities; 8) there will be reduced demand for office space in cities; and 9) new urban design standards will need to be introduced.[31] These are all important.

Here, taking a strategic approach, I identify five overarching policy issues, or dilemmas, that now require the attention of international, national and local leaders.

Policy issue 1: lives versus livelihoods

First, there is the so-called 'lives versus livelihoods' tension. This dilemma has been particularly visible in countries that have introduced lockdowns in response to COVID-19. Stated crudely, this is sometimes presented as a 'health versus the economy' choice. Some take the view that there is a straight-forward tension between the public health objective of saving lives, and the economic objective of helping to get businesses going again and to get people back into their jobs.

In truth, the choices are altogether more complex. Steps to bring people back to work could well have important health benefits, while keeping people healthy and safe can be expected to have significant economic benefits. Clearly, the debate about the interplay between economic and public health objectives needs to be thoughtful and sophisticated.

Policy issue 2: community versus individualism

Second, the COVID-19 challenge has sparked a truly spec-tacular increase in community activism, mutual aid and grassroots efforts to build social solidarity across the world. There are many thousands of inspiring examples, including the NHS volunteer scheme, launched in England on 24 March 2020. For a period, it was attracting volunteers at the rate of nearly five people per second, and over 750,000 people signed up to help within five days. This was three times as many as were expected, and the government had to pause the scheme in order to process the avalanche of messages offering help.

This outpouring of civic commitment has been replicated in volunteer centres across the country. This is on top of the remarkable growth, largely off the national radar, of informal mutual aid organizations that have sprung up in neighbourhoods, towns and villages across the UK. Of course, similar inspiring, community-based initiatives have flourished across the world.

This raises some big questions. Is this a signal that societies are now recognizing that social solidarity is vital for the future wellbeing of everyone? Or will this enthusiasm for community building come to be experienced as a temporary phenomenon, one that gives way to a reassertion of selfish individualism?

Policy issue 3: environmentalism versus economic growth at all costs

A third policy issue arising from the pandemic, and this could be described as a silver lining, is that there has been a startling environmental upside. Jonathan Watts explains how, after decades of rising pressure, the human footprint on earth was lightened significantly by COVID-19.[32] Global air traffic had halved by mid-March, compared with the same time in 2019. Motorway traffic virtually disappeared in many countries. Carbon emissions across the world dropped significantly. The residents of cities, particularly in developing countries, suddenly discovered what breathing fresh air felt like. Newspapers published striking 'before' and 'after' pictures of urban settings, revealing how COVID-19 had removed dense smog, in cities like Delhi and Beijing, and created a crystal clear, even alpine atmosphere.

In countries experiencing a lockdown, wildlife moved into the spaces vacated by human beings – coyotes were spotted on the Golden Gate Bridge in San Francisco, and goats appeared to enjoy roaming around Welsh towns like Bangor and Llandudno.

It would be foolish to believe that the environmental gains delivered by COVID-19 are secure. The fossil fuel industries, including the aviation companies, moved quickly to seek government bailouts, and they attracted massive financial support, notably in the US. Will COVID-19 put the brakes on endless resource consumption and spur radical action in relation to global warming? Or will the opportunity to engage in a rethink be missed?

Policy issue 4: civil liberties versus state control of behaviour

A fourth challenge concerns the balance to be struck between civil liberties and state surveillance. There is a genuine dilemma here, one that deserves much more examination. In many countries, national governments have, in order to stem the spread of COVID-19, passed draconian laws designed to extend state control over their people. For example, in the UK context, after the national lockdown was imposed on 23 March 2020, British police officers found that they were no longer merely guardians of the law. Rather, they were now also expected to interpret the changing, and somewhat ambiguous, national guidance tumbling out of Whitehall about 'social distancing' and the like. They were, in effect, being expected to monitor and control the daily behaviour of citizens. To be fair, the new measures had to be introduced very quickly, but this haste resulted in a significant downside. Some police forces, well intentioned or not, overstepped the mark by, for example, using drones to shame walkers in a deserted national park and, in some cases, inspecting the contents of people's shopping bags, to ascertain whether particular trips outside the home really were to purchase 'essential' items.

In practice, the COVID-19 pandemic has led to a truly massive global expansion of digital surveillance. The changed climate has opened up lucrative new markets for the global companies that had already developed highly sophisticated ways of extracting profit from our personal data, an abomination exposed by Shoshana Zuboff in her forensic analysis of 'surveillance capitalism.'[33] Naomi Klein has explained how the Silicon Giants, examples of the place-less, unaccountable power holders I described in Chapter One, are seizing every opportunity opened up by the pandemic to expand their reach, power and profits.[34]

The key challenge here, as explained by Shami Chakrabati in her book on civil liberties, is to be alert to the fact that measures introduced in a crisis (Baroness Chakrabati was referring in particular to the UK Terrorism Act 2000), may not be as well thought through as needs to be the case.[35] She rightly draws attention to the risk that laws passed in a crisis can result in intrusive surveillance being left in place long after a given emergency has passed. It is worth recalling the phrase, often attributed to an 1852 speech by Wendell Phillips, the American anti-slavery campaigner: 'Eternal vigilance is the price of liberty'.

Policy issue 5: tackling inequality versus forgetting about it

The fifth policy issue, and it is the most important one, is that COVID-19 is having a massively uneven impact on different groups in society. In one sense, it is right to claim that 'We are all in this together'; COVID-19 is a threat to all of us. But it is also true that COVID-19 discriminates in a brutal way. It is proving to be very effective in really hurting the people in society who are already vulnerable. This is not, of course, a feature of the virus. Rather, the virus is revealing, in a way that no amount of social scientific research could match, just how unequal societies had become well before the arrival of COVID-19. For example, the UK Office for National Statistics disclosed that people living in the poorest areas in England and Wales were, in the period from 1 March to 17 April 2020, dying at twice the rate of those living in less deprived areas.[36] In the 10 per cent least deprived areas, the death rate from COVID-19 was 25.3 per 100,000 people, compared with 55.1 per 100,000 people in the 10 per cent most deprived.

The UK Trades Union Congress (TUC) has published evidence showing the serious flaws in how the UK economy works:

> The crisis has shown who really keeps the country going – and also just how poorly paid many of our key workers are. It has also revealed the scale and depth of inequality in our country, with women, disabled people and Black and Minority Ethnic (BME) workers more likely to be affected because they are disproportionately stuck in insecure jobs on low pay.[37]

This TUC report puts forward suggestions on how to address these inequalities.

In countries experiencing lockdown, people in lower socio-economic groups have had to go out to work for reasons of economic necessity, even though this means that they then run the risk of becoming infected. Poorer, less well-educated people might also be less aware of social distancing guidelines and public health advice. Also, how do you self-isolate when you live in overcrowded accommodation or an informal settlement in a developing country? As Rebecca Solnit put it:

> What sheltering in a place means for the impoverished, overcrowded majority in some parts of the world is hard to fathom. What does a family of eight do in two rooms with a dirt floor, little food on hand, and no running water?[38]

The tragic death statistics published in the US have drawn attention to long-established racial inequalities. Afua Hirsch explains how COVID-19 is disproportionately affecting black communities. Writing in April 2020, she presents figures showing that in, for example, Chicago, while African Americans comprised 30 per cent of the population, they accounted for 70 per cent of the COVID-19 deaths in the city.[39] In Louisiana it was very similar: 32 per cent of the population is black, while black people made up 70 per cent of those who had died from COVID-19.

According to data published by the US Centers for Disease Control and Prevention on 17 April 2020, 30 per cent of COVID-19 patients in the US were African American, while African Americans made up only 13 per cent of the entire population. These figures are quoted in a devastating report on racial disparities in the US published by the Senate Democratic Policy and Communications Committee.[40]

This solid evidence of racial injustice provided the backdrop to the massive public protests against racism and police brutality that took place following the death of George Floyd in Minneapolis, US. On 25 May 2020, Floyd, a 46-year-old black man, died while being arrested by four police officers. Derek Chauvin was charged with second-degree murder and the other three officers involved were charged with aiding and abetting murder. The public outrage has led not just to proposals for reforming police authorities and police accountability in the US, but also to wide-ranging international campaigns to tackle racism head on.[41]

Just about everybody on the planet has been, or will be, affected by the COVID-19 pandemic. But we are not all affected in the same way. The astonishing differences in impact, revealed by the appalling death statistics, reflect the fact that most societies in the world have become unacceptably unequal in recent years.

Conclusions

This chapter has suggested that the rather grand words often used by policy makers and journalists to describe the COVID-19 pandemic – words like catastrophic, seismic, world-shaking – are well chosen. Billions of people have had their lives disrupted, millions have been infected and, as at 1 July 2020, some 514,000 people had died. Moreover, COVID-19 is not going to disappear – it will continue to pose a major threat to the health and wellbeing of all of us.

COVID-19 lays down, then, an unprecedented challenge to societies across the world and, in particular, it poses a challenge to the current arrangements we use for governing ourselves. Even at this relatively early stage in the COVID-19 story, we can see that politicians – and, indeed, scientists and experts – have been found wanting. Lives have been lost, because many governments were not as well prepared as they should have been before the disease emerged. Further lives have been lost because many governments made thoroughly bad decisions in their efforts to respond to the COVID-19 threat.

This chapter has shown that the challenges posed by COVID-19 for governance are extremely complex. It has also identified various policy issues or dilemmas that policy makers and society must now wrestle with. These policy issues concern matters that go well beyond public health and economics, and they are dilemmas that cannot be wished away. The central theme to emerge from this analysis, and it is one that will be developed in the rest of this book, is that governance matters. Without radical improvements in governance, we are all sitting ducks for the next pandemic. It is to the question of governance that we turn in the next chapter.

Notes

[1] For more details on the coronavirus, see: Mosley M. (2020) *COVID-19: What you need to know about coronavirus and the race for a vaccine*, London: Short Books.

[2] Maron D. F. (2020) 'Wet markets likely launched the coronavirus. Here's what you need to know', National Geographic, 16 April.

[3] Yu V. (2020) 'Hero who told the truth: Chinese rage over coronavirus death of whistleblower doctor', *The Guardian*, 7 February.

[4] Spinney L. (2020) 'Is factory farming to blame for coronavirus?', *The Guardian*, 28 March.

[5] Wallace R. (2016) *Big Farms Make Big Flu*, New York: Monthly Review Press.

[6] See Spinney (2020) (Note 4).

[7] Honigsbaum M. (2020) *The Pandemic Century: A history of global contagion from the Spanish flu to COVID-19*, London: Penguin.

[8] For more information on the campaign to get rid of factory farming, visit the Compassion in World Farming website: https://www.ciwf.org.uk/

[9] WHO (2020) '2019-nCov outbreak is an emergency of international concern', 31 January. https://www.euro.who.int/en/health-topics/health-emergencies/international-health-regulations/news/news/2020/2/2019-ncov-outbreak-is-an-emergency-of-international-concern

[10] Ghebreyesus T.A. (2020) *WHO Director-General's opening remarks at the media briefing on COVID-19*, 11 March, Geneva: WHO.

[11] WHO (2020) 'WHO Director-General's remarks at the media briefing on COVID-19', 16 March. https://www.who.int/dg/speeches/detail/who-director-general-s-opening-remarks-at-the-media-briefing-on-covid-19---16-march-2020

[12] The Worldometer website is: https://www.worldometers.info/coronavirus/?utm_campaign=homeAdUOA?Si

[13] The discussion in this chapter concentrates on the performance of Ministers in Westminster and officials in Whitehall. In practice the devolved administrations for Scotland, Wales and Northern Ireland have, to some extent, adopted somewhat different strategies and a future public inquiry will want to examine the nature and impact of these variations.

[14] National Audit Office (2018) *Adult Social Care at a Glance*, July, London: National Audit Office.

[15] Local Government Association (2018) *Local Government Funding: Moving the conversation on*, London: Local Government Association.

[16] These figures refer to the number of people given a three-day emergency food parcel by the Trussel Trust. If the many independent emergency food providers are included, it is estimated that the food parcel figure

for 2018–19 exceeded 2 million. For a detailed analysis of foodbanks, see: Garthwaite K. (2016) *Hunger Pains: Life inside foodbank Britain*, Bristol: Policy Press. For a moving account of the extreme hardships faced by those living in poverty, see *I, Daniel Blake*, a film directed by Ken Loach and released in 2016.

[17] Lawrence E., McIntyre N. and Butler P. (2020) 'Revealed: How austerity hit Labour areas hardest', *The Guardian*, 22 June.

[18] Pegg D., Booth R. and Conn D. (2020) 'Ministers were warned in 2017 of care home risk', *The Guardian*, 8 May.

[19] Toynbee P. and Walker D. (2020) *The Lost Decade 2010–2020*, London: Guardian Books.

[20] Toynbee and Walker (2020, p 312) (see Note 19).

[21] Alston P. (2018) *Statement on Visit to the United Kingdom*. Report of the Special Rapporteur, 16 November, Geneva: Office of the United Nations High Commissioner on Human Rights.

[22] Marmot M., Allen J., Boyce T., Goldblatt P. and Morrison J. (2020) *Health Equity in England: The Marmot Review 10 years on*, London: The Health Foundation.

[23] Marmot, M. (2020) 'A decade of austerity made England easy prey for COVID-19', *The Guardian*, 11 August.

[24] McInroy N. (2020) 'Coronavirus response points to future local government role', *Local Government Chronicle*, 19 March.

[25] Richard Horton, quoted in Sample I. (2020) 'UK failures over COVID-19 will increase death toll, says leading doctor', *The Guardian*, 18 March. See also Horton R. (2020) *The COVID-19 Catastrophe: What's gone wrong and how to stop it happening again*, Cambridge: Polity Press.

[26] McKie R., Helm T. and Savage M. (2020) 'Top scientists: Cummings has broken trust in COVID policy', *The Observer*, 31 May.

[27] Anthony A. (2020) 'Q and A with Anthony Costello', *The Observer*, 5 July, p 28.

[28] Rittel H. and Webber M. (1973) 'Dilemmas in a general theory of planning', *Policy Sciences*, 4(2): 155–169.

[29] Grint K. (2010) 'Wicked problems and clumsy solutions: The role of leadership', in S. Brookes and K. Grint (eds) *The New Public Leadership Challenge*, Basingstoke: Palgrave, pp 169–186.

[30] Bolden R. (2020) 'Leadership, complexity and change: Learning from the COVID-19 pandemic', 27 March, Bristol Leadership and Change Centre blog, University of the West of England, Bristol. https://blogs.uwe.ac.uk/leadership-and-change/leadership-complexity-and-change-learning-from-the-covid-19-pandemic/

[31] Muggah R. and Ermacora T. (2020) 'Redesigning the COVID-19 city', National Public Radio (NPR) Opinion article, 20 April. https://www.npr.org/2020/04/20/839418905/opinion-redesigning-the-covid-19-city

32 Watts J. (2020) 'Environmental upside: Nature has bounced back, but how long can it last?', *The Guardian*, 10 April.

33 Zuboff S. (2019) *The Age of Surveillance Capitalism*, London: Profile Books.

34 Klein N. (2020) 'How big tech plans to profit from the pandemic', *The Guardian*, 19 May.

35 Chakrabarti S. (2014) *On Liberty*, London: Allen Lane.

36 Pidd H., Barr C. and Mohdin A. (2020) 'UK's corona divide', *The Guardian*, 2 May.

37 Williamson J. (2020) *A Better Recovery: Learning the lessons of the corona crisis to create a stronger, fairer economy*, May, London: TUC. https://www.tuc.org.uk/ABetterRecovery?page=1

38 Solnit R. (2020) 'Coronavirus does discriminate, because that's what humans do', *The Guardian*, 17 April.

39 Hirsch A. (2020) 'The risk factor no one wants to talk about', *The Guardian*, 9 April.

40 Senate Democratic Policy and Communications Committee (2020) *Racial Disparities on Full Display: COVID-19 is disproportionately affecting communities of color*, 30 April, Washington, DC: Senate DPCC.

41 The Black Lives Matter movement provides more information: https://blacklivesmatter.com

THREE

The Central Challenge: Improving Governance

Introduction

Coming into operation on 5 July 1948, the British National Health Service (NHS) has been a much-loved public institution for over seventy years. A YouGov public attitude survey, carried out in 2018, showed that 87 per cent of UK citizens are proud of the NHS, a positive approval rating only topped at the time by the fire brigade with 91 per cent.[1] Given the remarkable and selfless way in which doctors, nurses and all health service workers have responded to the COVID-19 pandemic, it would not be surprising to discover that the NHS has now broken all British records for public service esteem. For ten weeks after the lockdown was announced on 23 March 2020, millions of British citizens, on each Thursday evening at 8 pm, stood at their doors and windows to applaud NHS staff and other essential workers. Public support for the NHS has, surely, never been higher.

The visionary founding principles of the NHS are that health services should be comprehensive, universal and free at the point of delivery. How did this extraordinary new service come to be created? In a nutshell, the Labour Party won a landslide victory in the 1945 general election and Aneurin Bevan, the newly appointed Minister of Health, was charged with establishing a new kind of health service. Bevan deserves the highest praise for pursuing his vision with great energy, negotiating cleverly with the various vested interests and pushing through the legislation.[2]

Winston Churchill and the Conservative Party voted *against* Bevan's National Health Service Bill in both April and July 1946 (at the second and third readings on the bill). This is worth highlighting, because Boris Johnson, the current UK Prime Minister, asserts that the Conservative Party is 'the party of the NHS', a false claim that is flatly contradicted by the historical record. The Conservative Party, as well as opposing the creation of the NHS in 1946, consistently failed to provide adequate funding for the NHS when in government in the 2010–19 period. As explained in Chapter Two, when COVID-19 appeared on the world scene in January 2020, the NHS was already on its knees as a direct result of damaging Conservative Party policies and spending cuts.

The main point I want to highlight from the creation of the NHS is that this world-leading public innovation, one that transformed British thinking about the role of the state in modern society, was conceived during the Second World War, when the UK was in dire straits. Moreover, after the Second World War, the country faced extraordinary financial difficulties. Not surprisingly, some felt that the time was not right for a massive expansion of a new welfare state. But this innate conservatism was swept aside.

It is, of course, true that a major crisis in society can give birth to fearful and unadventurous ways of thinking but – and this is the key point – it can also open up new vistas. Times of great social disruption can create the political space within which leaders advocating far-reaching, even unheard of, reforms may be able to attract support and gain momentum. Bevan and his colleagues understood this, and the way they exploited this political space with such skill in 1945 and 1946 provides a masterclass in how to bring about progressive reform. As suggested in Chapter One, the COVID-19 pandemic presents a similar political choice today. Will societies react in a defeatist and cautious way? Or will we see bold acts of political imagination that reshape the role of the state in modern society?

In this chapter, I will develop the argument that the most important challenge arising from the COVID-19 pandemic does not relate to medical treatments, vaccines, epidemiology, or even public health policies. These are all very important, but COVID-19 raises a much more fundamental question: how should we govern ourselves? The first duty of government in a democratic society is to protect and safeguard the lives of its citizens. As outlined in Chapter Two, soaring infection and death rates arising from COVID-19 demonstrate that, in 2020, many governments around the world, including the UK government, have comprehensively failed this basic test of their legitimacy.

It follows that it makes sense to bring a critical eye to the governing systems we have created and, if we can, identify some practical ways of improving the quality of our democratic arrangements for making public policy. The evidence suggests that governance needs improving at all levels – international, national and city/local. While this book is focused on how to improve city and local governance, this discussion must be situated within a full recognition of the need to improve multi-level governance in modern societies – just improving one level won't cut it.

First, the chapter considers the shift from government to governance that has taken place in many countries in recent years. The discussion then draws attention to the current global climate emergency. If governments fail to respond to this challenge, the future will be unbearably bleak. I then look afresh at how the COVID-19 pandemic is reshaping how we think about the role of the modern state in caring for its citizens and caring for the planet. In recent months, many countries across the world have prioritized public purpose and have intervened in both society and the economy to an extraordinary degree. These bold innovations have shifted the window of political possibilities. I will explore what all this might mean for the future.

From government to governance

Over the last twenty years or so, numerous writers have suggested that many countries have moved from an era of government to one of governance, and that this shift is happening at all levels of government.[3] The modern literature on the changing nature of governance is rich and varied, and there are differences of view about the desirability of this shift. But what exactly do these words mean? *Government* refers to the formal institutions of the state. Government makes decisions within specific administrative and legal frameworks, and uses public resources in a financially accountable way. Most importantly, government decisions are backed by the legitimate hierarchical power of the state.

Governance, on the other hand, involves government *plus* the looser processes of influencing and negotiating with a range of public and private agencies to achieve desired outcomes. A governance perspective recognizes the importance of collaboration between the public, private and non-profit sectors to achieve mutual goals. While the hierarchical power of the state does not vanish, the emphasis in governance is on influencing and coordinating the actions of others. A governance perspective recognizes that the state cannot go it alone.

A word of caution is needed here. This movement from government to governance is unfolding in different ways in different countries and contexts. For example, the emergence of urban governance in developing countries has had a different trajectory than in developed countries.[4] The long-established existence of the informal city, operating outside any regulatory framework and led by non-state actors, in many developing countries means that it is unwise to imply that the transition from government to governance is an appropriate way to characterize changes in approaches to city or local government in all countries.

Nevertheless, it is possible to generalize, and to say that the COVID-19 pandemic has brought forth a remarkable shift towards 'governance' ways of thinking at the national level in many countries, as well as in cities and localities within these countries. This is because there has been a rapid expansion in the number of efforts bringing together the public, private and non-profit sectors to serve public purpose. COVID-19 is, then, spurring us to think afresh about the relationships between the state, markets and civil society.

So far, so good. But what do we mean by *civil society*? Marilyn Taylor provides a useful overview of the long and distinguished history of the concept, and she also provides a helpful introduction to related terms – for example community, communitarianism, social capital and mutuality.[5] She explains how in Europe, with the collapse of feudal society, the idea of civil society emerged out of the separation of the realm of the state from the realm of the private. She suggests that civil society provides a foundation for reciprocity, mutuality and cooperation beyond the calculus of pure exchange. Billie Oliver and Bob Pitt emphasize the practical implications of this understanding:

> … the norms and values of a civil society are embodied in voluntary associations where skills of co-operation are developed. In political terms, a return to civil society calls for a return to a manageable scale of social life emphasising voluntary associations, churches and communities.[6]

Note here the reference to 'a manageable scale of social life'. The COVID-19 emergency has reminded us that reciprocity, cooperation, association, connection, solidarity, community – the building blocks of civil society – are largely place-based and local.

Taking account of these complexities, Figure 3.1 suggests that it is helpful to present the relationships between civil society, markets and the state as three overlapping spheres of influence. The diagram uses dotted lines to signal the way ideas flow between these sectors. The borders between these concepts are clearly porous and, indeed, some actors may find themselves operating in more than one sector at the same time.

This is, of course, a very simple conceptualization. It should be recognized that there are many competing voices within each of these three sectors. Also, within any given society, the balance of influence among these three spheres of influence will be uneven and will be subject to change over time. Some will say that the circles need to be different sizes to illuminate the power structure in their particular country, and they would be right. However, the diagram does not aim to illustrate actual power relations. Rather, it operates at a conceptual level and it can, perhaps, help us to think new thoughts about how these sectors may be able to work more effectively together.

In the modern world, there are few countries where these relationships are fixed and stable. Indeed, the COVID-19 pandemic has shown how the balance of importance among these three sectors can, as a matter of political choice, be dramatically transformed within a very short space of time. Take the UK. Announced on 20 March 2020, by Rishi Sunak, the Chancellor,

Figure 3.1: Civil society, markets and the state

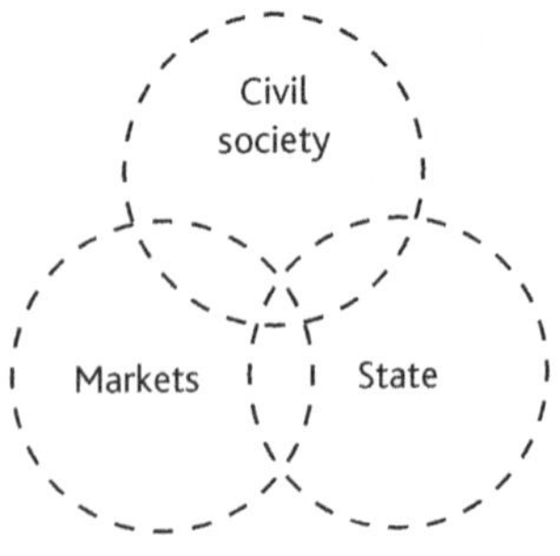

Source: Hambleton R. (2015), p 69

the British government introduced a 'furlough scheme' – officially called the Coronavirus Job Retention Scheme – to help employers pay their workers during the lockdown. In effect, this arrangement involved the state paying 80 per cent of the salary of workers up to a maximum of £2,500 a month. As a result, during April, nearly a quarter of British employees were furloughed. This meant that the state was, by 12 May 2020, paying the salaries of 7.5 million workers who had been temporarily laid off by 900,000 companies, with the cost amounting to £10 billion at that point. This represents a remarkable expansion of state support to needy citizens. In order to protect the quality of life of citizens, as well as the British economy, the size of the state circle in Figure 3.1 burgeoned. Post COVID-19 recovery plans will need to consider afresh what the future relationships between civil society, markets and the state should be.

Recognizing the global climate emergency

As mentioned in Chapter Two, the COVID-19 pandemic has had a startling impact on our environment. In a matter of weeks, global demand for energy dropped off a cliff. Air traffic was drastically reduced, and newspapers and other media outlets enjoyed publishing pictures of deserted motorways from Los Angeles to Shanghai. As carbon emissions plummeted, air quality in cities leapt *up* a cliff, reaching alpine levels of purity in many urban areas. There are hopes that, as societies recover from the COVID-19 onslaught, serious steps will be taken to hold onto these environmental gains, and that future policy will promote clean energy, green jobs and lifestyles that tread more lightly on the planet.

In Chapter Two, it was noted that steps to prevent future pandemics can, and should, be closely aligned with efforts to tackle climate change. For example, reducing meat consumption, doing away with factory farms and reducing food miles would all deliver major health and environmental benefits, as well as societal resilience. We can expect measures of this kind to be resisted by the industrialized agriculture companies as well as the fossil fuel industries. These vested interests will need to learn that the existence of planetary limits means that our future cannot be built on endless resource consumption.

This struggle to protect public health and the natural environment is not a new one. *Silent Spring*, Rachel Carson's farsighted analysis of the negative impacts of pesticides on the natural environment, was published in 1962.[7] Millions of environmental campaigners have followed in her footsteps, and societal understanding of the impact of misguided human action on the natural environment is now as highly developed as it has ever been. Caring properly for the natural environment raises many challenges for governance. Tim Jackson, in his 2009 book *Prosperity Without Growth*, as well as exposing the limitations of mainstream thinking in economics, offers helpful insights on the future of governance. He states:

> The role of government is to provide the capabilities for its citizens to flourish – within ecological limits … [This] entails shifting the balance of existing institutions and structures away from materialistic individualism and providing instead real opportunities for people to pursue intrinsic goals of family, friendship and community.[8]

Clearly responding to the current planetary climate crisis needs to be central to any future post COVID-19 strategy for governance. We need, somehow, to bring our relationships with nature into the heart of this conversation. In Figure 3.2, I present a simple framework developed by Richard Rees, a British urban designer, as it helps to bridge the divide between social scientific and ecological perspectives.[9]

Rees argues that the essential elements of contemporary life – the individual, society and nature – have become separated out, and that they need to be reconnected. Figure 3.2, derived from his perspective, illustrates a simple way of framing our thinking about sustainable living and sustainable development.[11] Dotted

Figure 3.2: The individual, society and nature

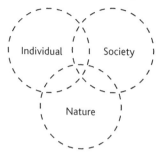

Source: Richard Rees, urban designer, UK[10]

lines are, again, used to signal that the boundaries are porous. Consistent with a growing body of writers on resilient cities and communities, Rees argues that city leaders, urban planners, architects, designers and others need to embed a fruitful co-existence with nature into urban policy and practice.[12] The philosophical underpinnings for this approach – which envisages a move from anthropocentrism to eco-centrism – are well established in green political thought.[13]

My purpose in presenting these two conceptual frameworks – one showing civil society/state/market relationships, the other illustrating individual/society/nature relationships – is to provide a backdrop to the more specific argument that now follows about the need to rethink the role of the state in modern societies. However, aside from that, I hope that these diagrams can help to stimulate fresh thinking about the interplay between the state, markets, nature, civil society and the individual.

Steering a progressive path

In the UK, over the last forty years or so, there have been major political disagreements, not just within Westminster but also within society at large, about the appropriate role of the state. Stated simply, in the late 1980s, Margaret Thatcher and her supporters sought to roll back the power and influence of the state. They believed that public policy should emphasize the virtues of so-called 'free markets.' Moreover, they felt that public spending should be reduced and that many public services should be privatized. Opponents of Thatcherism argued that such policies would damage the welfare state, weaken the social security safety net, harm much-needed public services, lead to an unacceptable rise in social and economic inequality, and destroy the natural environment.

As discussed in Chapter One, Nobel Prize-winning economist Joseph Stiglitz established over thirty years ago that markets do not deliver economic efficiency.[14] In a similar vein, Ha-Joon Chang explains that there is no such thing as a 'free market':

> The free market doesn't exist. Every market has some rules and boundaries that restrict freedom of choice ... The usual claim by free-market economists that they are trying to defend the market from politically motivated interference by government is false. Government is always involved and those free-marketeers are as politically motivated as anyone.[15]

This is a crucial insight. Realizing that there is no such thing as an objectively defined 'free market' is the first step to gaining an understanding of power relations in modern society. The COVID-19 pandemic has spurred on governments across the world to make astonishing and highly visible interventions in markets. This has had the effect of revealing, in a rather vivid way, that governments and markets are, indeed, inextricably intertwined. Crisis or no crisis, political leadership and political judgement are constantly needed, to ensure that markets serve the public good.

It may be helpful to mention here how I am using the term 'progressive' in this book. Historically, progressivism is a political philosophy that supports social reform. But there is no agreed definition of this word, and different groups within progressive politics have a range of aims and objectives. In my 2015 book *Leading the Inclusive City*, taking account of the urgency of the global climate crisis, I defined an inclusive city as one in which 'all residents are able to participate fully in society and the economy, and civic leaders strive for just results while caring for the natural environment on which we all depend'.[16] Following Rees (see Figure 3.2), I included the natural environment in my definition of inclusion. The suggestion here is that inclusion, as a policy objective, should be expanded beyond social, economic and democratic inclusion to embrace caring for the environment. A progressive society is, then, in my view, an inclusive society – it is characterized by a participatory approach to decision making and aims to advance social, economic and environmental justice.

COVID-19 and the role of the state

Owen Jones has provided a revealing account of the role of right-wing think tanks in reshaping political discourse about the role of the state in the period since the 1970s.[17] He explains how a variety of well-funded right-wing organizations – for example the Institute for Economic Affairs (founded 1955) and the Adam Smith Institute (1977), both based in the UK; and the Heritage Foundation (1973) and the Mackinac Center for Public Policy (1987) in the US – were very successful in shifting the political discourse towards the right in British and American politics.

Jones explains how these think tanks operated as 'outriders', extolling extremist, even dangerous, ideas that right-leaning politicians could then draw on. The influential, privately owned newspapers and media channels, in both the UK and the US, have trumpeted the views of these think tanks and continue so to do. Recall that the powerful press barons who control so much of our media are unsympathetic to both democracy and justice. These malign forces have an impact, but Jones adds an important insight:

It might seem tempting to view the outriders as nothing more than the tools of the wealthy elite, translating their economic interests into political ideas that are then peddled to the public ... [But these] ... ideological fellow travellers are not cynical charlatans, simply pumping out propaganda at the behest of powerful people. They are true believers, zealots even.[18]

It follows that the ideas and concepts promulgated by these think tanks should be examined, rather than dismissed out of hand.

In this context the Overton Window deserves our consideration. Named after Joseph P. Overton, the late vice-president of the Mackinac Center for Public Policy, based in Michigan, US, this window concept claims to describe what is politically possible or reasonable at any given time within the prevailing politics of the day. The window analogy is intended to describe a spectrum from 'more free' to 'less free' with regard to government intervention in society.

The window analogy is helpful as, in theory, it can provide a useful guide as to whether a particular idea has political viability or not. More important, the window analogy suggests that those seeking bold change, in whatever direction, need to think beyond the development of new policies. Radical reformers need to work out how to move the location of the window. Jones explains how the right-wing think tanks were able to shift the goalposts of political debate, in Britain and the US at least, making ideas that were once viewed as absurd into a strange new kind of 'common sense'.

The chief flaw with the Overton Window concept is that it misunderstands the nature of freedom. Those on the political right believe, in principle, that weak or minimal government is superior to strong government. This bias in thinking means that they assume, mistakenly, that reducing state intervention will just about always increase freedom. In terms of individual liberty there is, of course, something in this argument. To take a simple example, many laws relating to public safety force citizens to behave in particular ways. For example, laws requiring people to wear seat belts in vehicles, to not smoke in restaurants and bars, and to refrain from assaulting people who disagree with them are all laws that limit the freedom of individuals to do exactly what they want. There is, then, no doubt that the state can – and does – reduce the freedom of individual citizens. Note, however, that depending on the case in point, a well-designed restriction on individual freedom will bring societal benefits, in some cases enormous benefits. That aside, focusing attention only on individual freedom is a peculiarly narrow, even bizarre, way of conceptualizing what freedom actually means in the modern world.

The COVID-19 pandemic demonstrates, if more evidence were needed, that *some of our most important freedoms stem directly from strong collective action*. In recent months, societies across the world have favoured interventionist state action to meet the COVID-19 challenge, precisely *because they value freedom* – meaning freedom from sickness, freedom from poverty and freedom from death. It is difficult to imagine a freedom that should carry more weight than the freedom to live.

In this context, it is helpful to revisit the Beveridge Report of 1942, effectively the foundation stone of the British welfare state. Authored by William Beveridge (a Liberal), this influential report sought to free British citizens from five 'Giant Evils': squalor, ignorance, disease, want and idleness.[19] The Labour government of 1945–50 made progress in advancing many of these freedoms. In particular, it made a massive step towards creating freedom from disease, by creating our NHS.

A further argument against having a weak state is that it may, perhaps inadvertently, encourage bad practice. I have in mind here unscrupulous private sector interests that, for example, campaign for the freedom to pollute, the freedom to exploit people and the freedom to destroy forests and to induce a global environmental catastrophe. These interests do not, of course, use phrases like these in their campaigning. They prefer to describe wise government regulations designed to prevent pollution, protect worker rights and reduce carbon emissions as unnecessary 'red tape'.

Given that state intervention can both extend and reduce freedom, the Overton Window is using a metric – freedom – that points in opposite directions at one and the same time. This is a recipe for confused and faulty thinking. The COVID-19 pandemic has demonstrated that the Overton Window's conceptualization of 'freedom', always misconceived, is clearly fallacious.

Opening a new window of political possibilities?

Can we identify a better dimension than 'freedom' for assessing state intervention in society? Hopefully we can in the period ahead. It is clear that we need to open up new conversations designed to reconfigure future relationships between markets, the state, civil society and nature. As a contribution to these important conversations, I ask a question: might it be possible to build a useful measure of the performance of governance, by focusing on the concept of caring for others and for the planet?

In the first instance, I draw here on the work of Joan Tronto, a professor of political science at the University of Minnesota, who has argued that care, not economics, should be the central concern of democratic life.[20] In her radical analysis, she explains how caring, for ourselves and for others, should be the highest value that shapes the way we view the world. Life under lockdown highlights the wisdom of her analysis. During the COVID-19 emergency we have witnessed an extraordinary flourishing of caring and compassion in villages, communities, towns and cities across the world. Much of this benevolence has been directed at helping vulnerable, isolated and extremely poor people as well as immediate family, friends and neighbours. We have, then, witnessed a wonderful upsurge in human kindness.

If, following the discussion of inclusion outlined earlier, we add to this rise in caring for others a recognition that caring for the natural environment has also spiralled upwards in recent years, perhaps we have identified a unifying value for societal advance: *caring for others and the planet*. The COVID-19 pandemic has, to some extent, masked the fact that, alongside the seismic public health challenges arising from this nasty disease, we also face an ecological emergency. Recall that millions of people are, right now, actively campaigning to reduce carbon emissions, because they care about the natural environment, they care about the destruction of the lives of indigenous peoples as well as the obliteration of biodiversity and the alarming rise in global warming.

Figure 3.3 takes up this idea and outlines a new window of political possibilities, with caring for people and the planet on one side and encouraging unregulated markets and individualism on the other side. In this framework, individuals and communities aspiring to give priority to caring for people and the planet will strive to move the political window of possibilities to the left side of the diagram. People who are less concerned about these matters, and prioritize the promotion of unregulated markets and individualism, will want to see the political window moved to the right side of the diagram.

The COVID-19 pandemic has already prompted a rethink of the role of the state in many societies. The window of political possibilities is not just being rethought, it has already

Figure 3.3: A new window of political possibilities

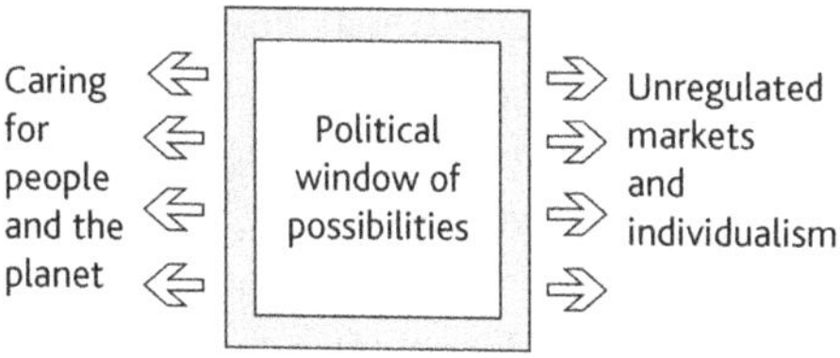

Source: Author

moved. Some countries have chosen to bail out companies, by giving financial support to businesses without attaching any socioenvironmental conditions – for example the UK 'furlough scheme', referred to earlier. However, some countries have realized that bailouts can provide a way of turning the dial away from the exploitation of people and planet. These countries are striving to shift the behaviour of companies in a far more responsible direction, one that prioritizes public purpose. Denmark provides a practical example of the kind of policies that can be pursued. In April 2020, the Danish government told companies that, if they were registered in tax havens, they would not be eligible for bailout funds to help them through the COVID-19 pandemic. The Danish government realizes that such companies have an out-of-date, exploitative model of behaviour, so they do not deserve societal support.

Mariana Mazzucato, a professor in economics of innovation and public value at University College London, has elaborated this argument. She suggests that governments should be very active in providing financial support to businesses that are in danger of going under as a result of the COVID-19 crisis. However, she rightly stresses that governments should not just give money away. Rather, the state should think strategically about the kind of society it wants to build in the post COVID-19 period and should impose conditions on the financial support it gives to businesses, in order to further its long-term strategic objectives.[21] There are real possibilities here, then, for moving the window of political possibilities towards a progressive vision of society.

The COVID-19 pandemic raises major challenges for governance at three levels: international, national and city/local. Here we consider each of these, very briefly, in turn. Before doing so, it is worth drawing attention to the importance of considering the transition process that will be needed to move from our current unsatisfactory governance arrangements to better ones in the future. In the UK, the Royal Society of Arts (RSA) has examined how this process of change could be handled and has put forward some interesting ideas on how to 'build bridges to the future'.[22] The RSA suggests that government should undertake rapid policy development and public engagement, to establish a framework for 'a year of stabilisation'. During this year, novel steps that have been introduced to develop short-term capacity to respond to the COVID-19 challenge can be assessed, to discover how they can be built on beyond the year of stabilization.

The international governance challenge

The performance of governments at the international level in responding to the COVID-19 challenge has been disappointing. Writing in *The Times*, Theresa May, the former Conservative Prime Minister of the UK, criticized world leaders for 'failing to forge a coherent international response'.[23] She expressed the view that an infectious new virus might seem to be just the thing that countries would want to work together on. This is not happening, and May warned that the global response risked 'exacerbating the shift towards nationalism and absolutism in global politics'.

The challenge facing us is clearly global, in the sense that nobody will be safe until the world is free of COVID-19. Gordon Brown, Labour Prime Minister of the UK at the time of the global banking crisis in 2008, is widely credited with playing a vital role in orchestrating the international response to the threat of imminent global economic collapse. There will be critics of the global decisions that were made. But there can be no denying that, at the time, the leading powers in the world came together to agree on a collaborative approach to stopping an impending calamity.[24]

In 2020, the system of international governance is altogether more fractured. Several important world powers appear to lack commitment to global governance, and President Trump has all but abandoned any interest in exercising American leadership on the world stage. On 14 April 2020, in a cynical attempt to distract attention from his own incompetence and dishonesty in dealing with the pandemic in the US, Trump announced that he was halting American contributions to the WHO. Government leaders and experts were dismayed and shocked at the US president's announcement, fearing that such a move would not only deprive the WHO of the resources it needs to fight the pandemic, but also undermine vital international collaboration between scientists.[25]

Founded straight after the Second World War, the United Nations (UN) brings together 193 member countries. While its main mission is to preserve international peace and promote human rights, it also strives to improve living standards by providing financial support to poor nations. In my view, the UN has, notwithstanding its many remarkable achievements in the last 75 years, never been more important. In March 2020, the UN published an exceptionally clear global report on COVID-19, one that has not received the recognition it deserves.[26] This study demonstrates, with evidence and insight, that the COVID-19 crisis is much more than a health crisis – it is a human crisis. The report shows how any successful strategy for responding to the challenges we now face, at a global level, needs to be linked directly to the delivery of the recent, globally agreed Sustainable Development Goals (SDGs). The report draws attention to political leadership (a topic we will explore in more detail in Chapter Four), and notes: 'At the geopolitical level, this crisis cries out for leadership, solidarity, transparency, trust and cooperation. This is no time for self-interest, recrimination, censorship, obfuscation or politicization. The tone set by leaders at the national and the local levels matters.'[27]

National governance responses: chalk and cheese

If we now turn to the national level, we can identify a wide range of responses. Countries that have done rather well in responding to the COVID-19 pandemic, as measured by number of deaths per head of population from the disease, include Hong Kong, New Zealand, Singapore, Australia and South Korea – see Table 2.2. The political leadership of a number of other countries has, however, been much less successful in containing the disease – see Table 2.1.

In Chapter Two, I provided an assessment of the performance of the UK government. This demonstrates that the leadership and judgement shown by the Conservative government, both before and after the COVID-19 outbreak, has been altogether poor. On 1 July 2020, the UK had recorded 43,730 deaths as a result of COVID-19, a figure that at the time was higher than any other European country. As measured by deaths per million, the UK (with 644 deaths per million) even outperformed the world leader in overall deaths from COVID-19 – the US (with 393 deaths per million).

As explained earlier in this chapter, right-wing political parties seek to shrink the power of the state, to cut public service budgets and to diminish the ability of governments to protect their citizens. The Conservative government mounted a ruthless and sustained attack on UK public services in the 2010–19 period, and this was bound to lead to a sharp increasing in human suffering, particularly for poor people. The COVID-19 pandemic delivers the unbearable result of such knowingly cruel and thoughtless public policies: more suffering and more deaths, particularly among the black and minority ethnic population. The forthcoming public and parliamentary inquiries into the performance of the UK Conservative government become more urgent with each passing day.

While the UK and other right-wing governments have weakened the role of the state in modern society, US President Donald Trump has taken the decimation of government to an appalling new level. Michael Lewis, in *The Fifth Risk*, provides a shocking account of how, from the very beginning, the Trump administration showed no interest in understanding how the federal government operated, still less in learning how to run it.[28] President Obama's administration, in line with the long-established practice of outgoing US presidents, prepared

meticulous transition documents for the incoming administration. These offered detailed briefings on, for example, services provided, relevant trends and the key issues facing each
department. Trump's incoming team had virtually no interest
in reading any of them.

Instead, Trump left hundreds of government positions
unfilled and appointed people to head up departments,
agencies and regulatory bodies who were unqualified and/
or had clear conflicts of interest. Trump's contempt for
democratic norms and his intolerable treatment of officials
has resulted in thousands of highly qualified people leaving
the federal government since 2017. It is, then, not surprising to discover that the Trump administration was totally
unprepared to lead and coordinate a national response to
the COVID-19 pandemic. Indeed, in September 2019 the
administration closed down Predict, a federal early warning
system designed to anticipate potential pandemics.[29] In a
recent analysis, drawing on detailed insider accounts, George
Packer suggests that, if Trump is elected for a second term,
the damage to US government and the US constitution
could be permanent.[30]

It is not surprising that Trump's shocking behaviour attracts
international headlines. But we should not allow this to distract
us from the fact that many national governments have reacted
to the global pandemic with wisdom and insight.

The power of the local

The evidence suggests that cities and local governments, across
the world, have, on the whole, responded well to the COVID-
19 pandemic. Municipal governments, working in partnership
with local health authorities and community leaders, business
leaders and other local stakeholders, have been on the front
line in dealing with this crisis. This is a tough place to be,
particularly in countries where higher levels of government
have cut funding to elected local authorities.

The evidence from local news coverage suggests that local leaders have been able to exercise a vital, even life-saving, civic leadership role in three mains ways: in directing citizens to accurate information; in taking action to address particular concerns relating to vulnerable groups in the population; and in working with a variety of civil society organizations and citizens to devise collaborative community-based solutions.[31] As explained in Chapter One, the power of place has been seriously undervalued in public policy in many countries and this needs to change.

The time is right to ask an important question: what is local government for? In my 2015 book, *Leading the Inclusive City*, I discuss this question at some length, and conclude that the overall purpose of local government is to provide place-based leadership for the common good.[32] Four more specific purposes are set out in that book:

- to defend our political liberties against a potentially auto-cratic central state and other external forces;
- to support a community-based approach to public service innovation, tapping local energies and resources;
- to provide outstanding public services to meet the needs of all residents and enhance the quality of life;
- to create eco-friendly, prosperous communities, able to adapt to changing circumstances.

The good news is that elected local authorities across the world have been pursuing these objectives with energy and enterprise for decades. More than that, recent years have seen an upsurge of innovations in local democracy that are developing new possibilities for extending both representative and participatory democracy. Subsequent chapters will explore the changing nature of local governance in more detail and, in particular, will discuss the role and potential of place-based leadership to help us co-create a post COVID-19 world that is guided by progressive values.

Conclusions

It seems clear that the COVID-19 pandemic will now spur on many societies to engage in a serious process of lesson drawing for the future. As a minimum, we can anticipate that many countries will decide to look afresh at the way they currently fund and support their health and social care systems. The avoidable human suffering that has taken place in hospitals and care homes for the elderly, as well as in the community at large, will surely reinforce the wisdom of putting more public funding into health and social care services. In this chapter, I have suggested that the COVID-19 pandemic does more than ask us to reconsider the value we place on health and social care services; the disease has drawn attention to startling levels of inequality that now pervade many modern societies and has raised fundamental questions about arrangements for self-governance.

Three related themes, or questions, emerge from the discussion presented in this chapter. First, does the COVID-19 pandemic provide an opportunity for bringing about positive transformative change in society? There is evidence to suggest that major societal disruptions do provide opportunities for significant changes to take place. In the introduction to this chapter, I explained how the creation of the British NHS immediately after the Second World War was an astonishing civic achievement. A country exhausted from six years of all-out war decided to embark on a major programme of societal reform. Perhaps it is too early to say whether the pandemic will have a galvanizing effect and encourage citizens and politicians to move their societies in a progressive direction. But the possibility is clearly available to us.

In this chapter, I have suggested that it may be possible for post COVID-19 recovery to unite large numbers of people behind three closely related agendas:

- improving the arrangements for keeping people healthy and safe;

- recognizing the urgency of the global climate emergency and the need for a green approach to regenerating the economy;
- developing a progressive agenda that tackles social and economic inequality, by putting inclusion centre stage in strategy and policy.

This may appear to be a utopian vision and I make no apology for that. Utopian thinking is often dismissed as offering idealistic and impractical proposals for social reform and/or radical change. This is to misunderstand the idea, however. I share the view expressed by John Friedmann, the famous city planner and social theorist, who argues that: 'If injustice is to be corrected … we will need the concrete imagery of utopian thinking to propose steps that would bring us a little closer to a more just world'.[33]

A second, closely related, theme concerns the role of the state. In this chapter, I have suggested that the COVID-19 pandemic raises fresh questions about the balance that societies should strike between the state, markets, nature, civil society and the individual. I have suggested that there is no such thing as a 'free market' – all states shape and control markets. Moreover, the evidence suggests that rolling back the state does not, in fact, lead to an increase in freedom from inequality, suffering, disease and similar societal evils. I have suggested that a new window of political possibilities is now opening up for us, one that seeks to guide government efforts by examining whether or not specific policies and practices advance, or hinder, the aim of caring for people and the planet – see Figure 3.3.

The third theme relates to the quality of governance. The chapter has shown that the international response to the governance challenge arising from COVID-19 has, on the whole, been poor. This needs to change. At the national level of governance, there is considerable variation in performance. More research is needed to discover what lessons we can draw from the countries that did particularly well in responding to the COVID-19 emergency. But, even in advance of that research, we already know that some national governments have performed badly. These countries should hold formal public inquiries to learn lessons for future policy and practice.

Turning to the city or local level of governance there is anecdotal evidence to suggest that this level of governance has, on the whole, performed relatively well in responding to the COVID-19 threat. It follows that it should be possible to study successful examples of local, collaborative leadership practices that existed well before COVID-19 disrupted so many people's lives, and draw lessons. Lastly, this chapter has shown that any future strategy for post COVID-19 recovery will need to enhance the quality of multi-level governance. Innovation at international, national and city/local levels is needed.

In Chapter One, I introduced the concept of the power of place and the importance of civic leadership. This chapter has explored the idea of governance in more detail and has raised some ideas about the possible future role of the state. In the next chapter, we focus on local governance and, in particular, the idea of place-based leadership.

Notes

[1] Smith M. (2018) *YouGov Public Attitude Survey*, 4 July.

[2] Much of the idea development that underpinned the creation of the British NHS and, indeed, the British welfare state was carried out during the Second World War. For more details, see: Willcocks A.J. (1967) *The Creation of the National Health Service*, London: Routledge and Kegan Paul; Timmins N. (2001) *The Five Giants: A biography of the welfare state* (2nd edn), London: Harper Collins.

[3] See, for example: Pierre J. and Peters B.G. (2000) *Governance, Politics and the State*, Basingstoke: Palgrave; Denters B. and Rose L.E. (eds) (2005) *Comparing Local Governance: Trends and developments*, Basingstoke: Palgrave; Davies J.S. (2011) *Challenging Governance Theory: From networks to hegemony*, Bristol: Policy Press; Levi-Faur D. (2012) 'From "Big Government" to "Big Governance"?' in D. Levi-Faur (ed) *The Oxford Handbook of Governance*, Oxford: Oxford University Press.

[4] McCarney P.L. and Stren R.E. (eds) (2003) *Governance on the Ground: Innovations and discontinuities in cities of the developing world*, Baltimore, MD: Johns Hopkins University Press.

[5] Taylor M. (2003) *Public Policy in the Community*, Basingstoke: Palgrave.

[6] Oliver B. and Pitt B. (2013) *Engaging Communities and Service Users: Context, themes and methods*, Basingstoke: Palgrave, p 56.

[7] Carson R. (1962) *Silent Spring*, Boston, MA: Houghton Mifflin.

[8] Jackson T. (2009) *Prosperity Without Growth: Economics for a finite planet*, London: Earthscan, p 169.

[9] Richard Rees and I spoke at a conference on *Places in Transition* in London on 21 January 2010, organized by the UK Resource for Urban Design Information. I draw here, with his permission, on his presentation titled *Re-thinking Places: The individual, society and nature in city design.*

[10] I am grateful to Richard Rees for giving me permission to use this diagram.

[11] This framework departs from the familiar presentation of sustainable development in the literature and in public policy circles. The established model of sustainable development also comprises three overlapping spheres – but these are usually labelled as 'environmental', 'economic' and 'social'.

[12] See, for example: Berners-Lee M. and Clark D. (2013) *The Burning Question: We can't burn half the world's oil, coal and gas: So how do we quit?*, London: Profile Books; Wallace-Wells D. (2019) *The Uninhabitable Earth: A story of our future*, London: Penguin.

[13] Eckersley R. (1992) *Environmentalism and Political Theory: Toward an eco-centric approach*, London: UCL Press.

[14] See, for example: Stiglitz J.E. (1989) *The Economic Role of the State*, Oxford: Blackwell; and, more recently, Stiglitz J.E. (2020) *People, Power and Profits: Progressive capitalism for an age of discontent*, London: Penguin.

[15] Chang H. (2010) *23 Things They Don't Tell You About Capitalism*, London: Penguin, p 1.

[16] Hambleton R. (2015) *Leading the Inclusive City: Place-based innovation for a bounded planet*, Bristol: Policy Press, p 25.

[17] Jones O. (2014) *The Establishment: And how they get away with it*, London: Allen Lane.

[18] Jones (2014 pp 38–39) (see Note 17).

[19] Beveridge W. (1942) *Social Insurance and Allied Services*, Cmnd 6404, London: H.M. Government.

[20] Tronto J.C. (2013) *Caring Democracy: Markets, equality and justice*, New York: New York University Press. See also: Puig de la Bellacasa M. (2017) *Matters of Care: Speculative ethics in more than human worlds*, Minneapolis, MN: University of Minnesota Press.

21 Mazzucato M. (2020) 'Capitalism's triple crisis', *Social Europe*, 9 April.

22 Royal Society of Arts (RSA) (2020) *COVID-19: 'A year of stabilisation' to build bridges to the future*, 24 May, London: Royal Society of Arts.

23 May T. (2020) 'Nationalism is no ally in this battle without borders', *The Times*, 6 May.

24 Paulson H. (2010) *On the Brink*, London: Headline Publishing Group; Darling A. (2011) *Back from the Brink*, London: Atlantic Books.

25 Boseley S. (2020) 'Trump's cut to WHO funding is "dangerous and short-sighted"', *The Guardian*, 16 April.

26 United Nations (2020) *Shared Responsibility, Global Solidarity: Responding to the socio-economic impacts of COVID-19*. March. https://unsdg.un.org/sites/default/files/2020-03/SG-Report-Socio-Economic-Impact-of-Covid19.pdf

27 United Nations (2020 p 11) (see Note 26).

28 Lewis M. (2019) *The Fifth Risk: Undoing democracy*, London: Penguin Books.

29 Anthony A. (2020) 'A president usually leads. He's being dragged along', *The Observer*, 3 May.

30 Packer G. (2020) 'How to destroy a government', *The Atlantic*, April.

31 In the UK context, local authority responses to the COVID-19 emergency have been documented, in detail, by the two national local government magazines: *Local Government Chronicle* and *MJ* (Municipal Journal). See also these websites: Local Government Association (https://www.local.gov.uk) and Local Government Information Unit (https://lgiu.org)

32 Hambleton (2015 pp 173–203) (see Note 16).

33 Friedmann J. (2002) *The Prospect of Cities*, Minneapolis, MN: University of Minnesota Press, p 104. See also Friedmann J. (2000) 'The good city: In defence of utopian thinking', *International Journal of Urban and Regional Research*, 24(2): 460–472.

FOUR

The New Civic Leadership

Introduction

While the COVID-19 pandemic has brought about great suffering, particularly for disadvantaged families and individuals, it has also stimulated a remarkable upswing in mutual aid, community activism and caring behaviours. In countless cities and communities across the world, a blossoming of human kindness has led to the creation of many new forms of caring and help – from energetic new neighbourhood support networks, through fund raising for a multitude of different social projects, to teams of volunteers making face masks and surgical gowns for doctors, nurses and care workers. This extraordinary outpouring of goodwill is heart warming and, hopefully, we can build on this civic altruism in the future.

The importance of caring for others and creating inclusive forms of government to serve public purpose was recognized over 250 years ago by the philosopher Jean-Jacques Rousseau. Published in 1762, his far-sighted book *The Social Contract* provides many valuable insights on social solidarity and civic virtue, as well as a robust critique of selfish individualism. Rousseau was an early advocate of good governance, arguing: 'The better the state is constituted, the more does public business take precedence over private in the minds of the citizens'. For Rousseau, a successful society is one in which citizens care about other people and are actively engaged in the process of public decision making: 'As soon as public service ceases to be the main concern of the citizens and they come to prefer to serve the state with their purse rather than their person, the state is already close to ruin'.[1]

Rousseau is, in effect, saying that it is not enough to be law abiding and pay your taxes. Rather, in a well-run city-state – city-states were enormously important in his day – everyone 'hastens to the assemblies' and contributes to public life. Were he alive today, Rousseau would no doubt have great difficulty in comprehending the behaviour of the many modern multinational companies that seek to avoid paying appropriate taxes to the countries where their business activities are located. These companies do not even pass the most basic test of civic virtue. In Rousseau's terms, they are so uncaring that they are not even willing to 'serve the state with their purse'.

This chapter explores the idea of civic purpose, particularly as it relates to communities living in specific places. Alternative ways forward for public service reform in the post COVID-19 era will be considered. In the previous chapter, it was suggested that a new window of political possibilities could be opening up, one that recognizes that a purposeful state can expand rather than erode freedoms. Enhancing the capacity of the state to work with other actors in society to deliver freedom from disease and suffering, and to tackle the climate change emergency, raises complex issues. We will explore some of these and, in particular, we will consider what the implications are for public management and the co-creation of public services. Discussion then turns to consider the role of place and place-based leadership in responding to the multifaceted challenges thrown up by the COVID-19 pandemic. A way of conceptualizing modern place-based leadership is set out, and this will highlight the importance of co-creating collaborative governance arrangements at the city and locality level that can spur on public innovation and reinforce citizen participation.

Mapping the trajectories of public service reform

In this section, in an effort to identify reform options for our post COVID-19 future, we consider the way public service reform in the UK has unfolded over the last fifty years or so. As explained in Chapter Three, the creation of the British welfare state, after the end of the Second World War, was an impressive achievement. Over the next thirty years or so, public services expanded and the societal benefits were spectacular – life expectancy increased, educational opportunities boosted social mobility, the position of women in society was dramatically improved, national parks were introduced to protect some of our most exceptional environments, inequality in society was reduced, and there was a major expansion in vital public services, including education, housing, firefighting, and social care, not to mention the NHS.[2]

Notwithstanding these remarkable achievements, in the mid-1970s, questions were raised about the way the welfare state was working. In particular, were public services becoming too bureaucratic?[3] For each service there emerged: a defined department or division; an administrative hierarchy of control; a set of procedures designed to ensure uniformity of treatment; and groups of professionals or specialists to perform the tasks. While, at their best, such departments provided an impartial and fair service *for* the population, service users began to complain that they were often inflexible, and that they frequently displayed a 'we know best' attitude in their dealings with the public.

Discontent with this model of public service grew, and three main options for tackling bureaucratic paternalism emerged – see Figure 4.1. Starting at the bottom of the diagram, in the 1970s, we find large public service organizations staffed by professionals. Imbued with a strong commitment to public service, these professionals worked hard to provide services *for* people – and they tended to describe the people they served as 'clients'. The critique that emerged was that these organizations, while they were well meaning, often failed to connect adequately with the lived experience of service users.

The diagram identifies three routes to reform represented by three upward-facing arrows. The first broad alternative, shown on the left of Figure 4.1, rejects the very idea of collective and non-market provision for public need. Centring on the notion of privatization, it seeks to replace public provision with private provision – it strives to extend market models, particularly the idea of competition, into the realm of public services. We discussed the role of various right-wing think tanks in promoting these ideas in Chapter Three. Defenders of this strategy claim that, by enabling consumers to exercise choice between competing providers, these organizations will become more responsive.

The second alternative, shown on the right of Figure 4.1, aims to preserve the notion of public provision, but seeks a

Figure 4.1: Public service reform strategies

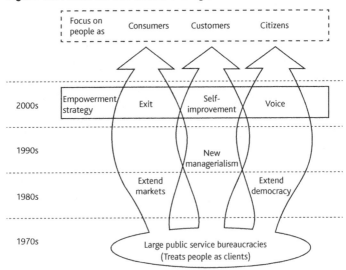

Source: Adapted from Burns D. et al (1994)[4]

radical reform of the manner in which this provision is under-taken. It seeks to extend, not reduce, democracy. It strives to replace the old, bureaucratic, paternalistic model with a much more democratic approach, one that envisages working *with* people rather than providing services *for* people.[5] This citizen-oriented approach to reform has led to a radical reshaping of the role of the third sector in many societies. The third sector – variously described as the 'voluntary sector' or the 'non-profit sector' – has become increasingly important in many societies.[6] A consequence is that the boundaries between the state and civil society are now blurred by the emergence of a class of organizational hybrids. There has, then, been a leap forward in co-production, co-management and co-governance.[7] In effect, the areas of overlap between the circles shown in Figure 3.1 have expanded.

Note that, as indicated at the top of Figure 4.1, the market approach treats people as *consumers* of services, and the democratic approach treats people as *citizens* with a right to be heard. The third broad strategy for public service reform, shown running up the centre of the diagram, has become increasingly influential in the last twenty years or so. It attempts to distinguish a managerial response from a political response to the problems confronting public service bureaucracies. This strategy borrows from the two competing political models in a way that simulates radical methods, but in a form that preserves existing power relations between the producers and users of services. In this model, citizens are redefined as *customers*.[8]

Understanding how empowerment works

The new window of political possibilities, introduced in Chapter Three, suggests that the relationships between the state, markets and civil society need to be looked at afresh. In essence there needs to be a shift towards caring for people and the planet – see Figure 3.3. What insights can we draw from this discussion of public service reform strategies for post COVID-19 recovery strategies?

Albert Hirschman, the famous economist and author, developed two ideal theoretical notions of empowerment – exit and voice – that can illuminate the important choices now opening up for societies.[9] He argues that members of an organization, a nation or any other form of human grouping, have essentially only two ways of responding to unsatisfactory performance: they can *exit* (withdraw from the relationship); or express their *voice* (in an effort to complain or set out proposals for change). Hirschman also has interesting things to say about a third concept – loyalty – but let's set that aside for the moment.

As Figure 4.1 implies, the power of exit is associated with the workings of markets – hence my use of the word *consumer* to describe the focus of this approach. In day-to-day life, this empowerment mechanism can work very well indeed. You go to a pub to meet some friends for a drink. The beer is not very good, so you exit this particular pub and go to another one. You have the substantial power of exit and it can be very effective. Voice, on the other hand, is by its nature political and, not surprisingly, ties in with the idea of the free *citizen* exercising the right to vote, protest, campaign, and so on. The concept of voice includes a wide range of political strategies – from petitions and mass demonstrations through to civil disobedience and direct action by citizens.

It is the exercise of voice, by concerned and/or oppressed citizens, that has underpinned social advance for centuries. The campaigns to win the right to vote for men and women in free and fair elections, the very existence of human rights and, of course, the creation of welfare states in Britain and elsewhere all stem from citizens making a stand against injustices and pressing for political change. Hirschman notes that, while both exit and voice can be used to assess organizational performance, voice is by nature more informative, in that it provides reasons why people are unhappy.

The third strategy for reform identified in Figure 4.1 – new managerialism – is not derived from Hirschman's work. This is because it is not, in fact, an empowerment mechanism at all. Rather, it comprises a managerial response to changing public pressures. In place of the unsettling signals of exit and voice, this approach reaches for private sector management techniques – market research, user satisfaction surveys, complaints procedures, customer care programmes, 'mystery shopping' visits, interactive websites, focus groups and the like.[10] This panoply of techniques is intended to provide more gentle and manageable feedback. The key point about feedback, as opposed to pressure, is that it doesn't force the organization to change – rather, it is about establishing a relationship with *customers* or, in management-speak, customer intimacy or even customer control.

If we now step back, we can distinguish 'four Cs' that can help us to understand the competing values that can be expected to influence post COVID-19 public service reform strategies. These words draw attention to the nature of the relationship between the state and the people it is there to serve. The 'four Cs' are:

- *Client* – This implies a dominance of the client by the professional and is the word that was often used in traditional public administration.
- *Consumer* – This implies a self-interested agent in the marketplace interested solely in the product or service provided. In Hirschman's terms, it is the consumer who has the economic power of exit.
- *Customer* – This implies giving attention to the experience of the person using the service of the organization and, ideally, building a relationship with that person.
- *Citizen* – This is someone who has a right to influence public decisions affecting the quality of life, and responsibilities in relation to other citizens. In Hirschman's terms, it is the citizen who has the political power of voice.

These distinctions about the words used to describe the way the state relates to the people it is there to serve are critical. We can, perhaps, take it that in the modern world, a state that treats people as 'clients' is using a rather out-of-date, paternalistic model. There are also serious problems with the market or 'consumer' perspective in a public service context. First, for many public services there is nowhere else to exit to. For example, it is ludicrous to suggest that a poor family can leave an area and relocate to another place that provides better housing and public services at the drop of a hat. Second, many public services are collectively produced and collectively enjoyed – for example public parks, playgrounds, streets, footpaths, cycle lanes, libraries and museums. The public benefit cannot be sliced into individual purchases. Third, the introduction of market mechanisms into public service provision can be viewed as an attack on the local polity in that, by fostering a self-interested and individualistic approach to decision making, it works against debate and deliberation about collective concerns and needs.

Amplifying citizen voice

A key lesson emerging from this discussion of the nature of empowerment is that progressive collaborative governance requires active citizen participation. To use Albert Hirschman's phrase, citizen voice needs to be amplified. The good news is that, in the last twenty years or so, community activists and elected local authorities across the world, as well as some nation states, have been experimenting with a remarkable diversity of approaches to citizen involvement, and these can be built on in the future. In the UK context, for example, Locality (a national network of community organizations) has, by drawing on the grassroots experience of its many members, provided helpful advice on how communities can help society to build a better post COVID-19 future.[11]

There are, of course, many ways of empowering citizens. We will discuss this topic further in Chapter Six, when we look at international experiences with innovations in local governance. Here, I mention just three noteworthy examples of citizen empowerment to prompt fresh thinking in relation to the development of post COVID-19 recovery plans.

Working with families

First, I highlight the imaginative work carried out by Participle, a UK social enterprise founded by Hilary Cottam.[12] Its approach sought to bring about a radical change in the relationships between the state and the people it is there to support. I first encountered Participle in 2010, when Jo Howard and I collaborated with Swindon Borough Council in an international project designed to advance understanding of public sector innovation.[13] We drew lessons from the Swindon Family LIFE programme, an approach that involves public service professionals working in an open and collaborative way with families experiencing chronic problems. In essence, the LIFE programme seeks to raise family self-esteem and capabilities. In this model, multi-service teams focus on coaching and empowering families, while also challenging families to think of new possibilities for themselves.[14]

Participatory budgeting

Second, participatory budgeting, which involves citizens in deciding directly how public money is spent, is now in use in a growing number of cities and localities. Porto Alegre, Brazil, should be credited with creating and implementing the first full participatory budget process in 1989. This empowerment strategy was seen to be highly successful. Capital spending in the city was redirected to focus on priorities identified by citizens – for example, sewer and water connections and schools.[15]

It was not surprising, therefore, that the approach spread rapidly to hundreds of Latin American cities, and we will refer to the experience of Mexico City in Chapter Six. In more recent years, participatory budgeting has been taken up by cities in Europe, North America and elsewhere.[16] There are now many varieties of participatory budgeting. A word of caution is needed. Some of the cities that claim to have adopted it have only introduced a pale imitation. For example, devolving comparatively small public budgets to neighbourhoods within a city can end up doing relatively little to enhance citizen power, and such action may even deflect public attention from more important matters. The original idea of participatory budgeting is radical. It involves citizens in having a direct say in decisions relating to a *significant* part of a municipal or public budget.

Citizens' assemblies

Third, citizens' assemblies also provide a route to citizen empowerment. The idea here is to create a new way of strengthening the voice of citizens, one that should sit alongside established democratic representative arrangements. Citizens' assemblies are not intended to replace the familiar architecture of political decision making found in democratic societies – free and fair elections, equal voting rights, majority rule, and so on. Rather, they are intended to improve that process of decision making. A citizens' assembly brings together people to deliberate on an issue of local or national importance and to offer proposals to those in power.[17] Details vary, but a key feature is that the members of a citizens' assembly are randomly selected. The aim is to ensure that all voices have an equal chance of being represented in the assembly. Generally speaking, a citizens' assembly strives to enhance the quality of deliberation about important issues, by including a diversity of voices. Three groups of people are usually involved: randomly selected citizens; expert witnesses; and facilitators or organizers. Typically, a citizens' assembly will work through three steps: learning (including taking evidence from expert witnesses); deliberation; and decision making. The model has been used at national level as well as at city/local government level. For example, in recent years the Citizens' Assembly of the Republic of Ireland has considered a number of political issues, including policies relating to abortion, climate change and the manner in which referenda are held.[18] The number of locally based citizen assemblies is also on the rise. For example, in 2018 the Extinction Rebellion environmental movement called for citizens' assemblies on climate change, and many have now been set up.[19]

The rise of New Public Management

Let's go back a step. In the UK and the US over the last forty years or so, as discussed in Chapter Three, right-wing think tanks have been energetic in promoting 'public is bad, private is good' ways of seeing and thinking – the precise opposite of the philosophy advocated by Jean-Jacques Rousseau. New Public Management (NPM), an approach that rests on the view that private sector management techniques, and ways of thinking, should be imported into the public sector, emerged in the 1990s to become an extremely influential force in public policy making in numerous countries.[20] Originally emanating from the UK, Australia and the US, the idea of trying to reconfigure public service bureaucracies as if they were private sector, or corporate, organizations spread across the world, and was particularly popular in industrialized countries.[21]

On the upside, NPM ideas spurred improvements in cost consciousness in many public bureaucracies and, in some cases, customer care concepts enhanced the experience of those seeking the support of public service providers. On the downside, NPM approaches eroded the long-established public service ethos, and the very idea of committed professionals serving public purpose was downgraded. The role of the state in caring for others and maintaining social cohesion was, in essence, seriously undervalued. Encouraged by Prime Minister Thatcher in the UK and President Reagan in the US, NPM ideas influenced the privatization, or quasi-privatization, of major public services in many countries. In a subtle, and not so subtle, way these ideas resulted in efforts to push the idea of profit-seeking behaviour as a new lodestar for public service managers.

Not surprisingly, NPM ideas and concepts soon came to be questioned. Various writers have shown that privatization, marketization, treating citizens as if they were self-interested consumers, and similar strategies, have serious limitations.[22] Henry Mintzberg, the respected Canadian professor of management studies, offered an early and particularly robust critique of NPM, arguing that to treat citizens as customers of public services is to completely misunderstand the nature of the relationship between people and their government.[23] Mintzberg was rightly pointing out that NPM does nothing to advance empowerment of the individual or collective rights. As shown in Figure 4.1, developing a customer orientation in public services, enhancing the capacity of staff to treat people in a thoughtful and empathetic way, is a good thing. But it is not an empowerment strategy, because the customer remains subservient. To use Hirschman's words, the power of exit is not available and the power of voice is muted.

During the last twenty years or so, policy makers in many countries, cities and localities have attempted to move on from the flawed concepts of NPM. These efforts have been documented and evaluated in two overlapping academic literatures: the literature on new public governance, public value and the co-production of public services[24]; and the literature on participatory democracy and citizen involvement.[25]

The ideas underlying New Civic Leadership

By learning from the experiences of some of the most innovative cities in the world, I have developed a New Civic

Leadership conceptual framework – presented in Figure 4.2.[26] This model is intended to offer a clear alternative to NPM, and to provide a fresh contribution to the literatures on new public governance, co-production and participatory democracy.

The four key ideas underlying the New Civic Leadership are:

- the need to recognize and expand the power of place;
- the importance of activists and policy makers moving beyond 'public' to embrace 'civic' as a way of thinking;
- the urgency of switching attention from 'management' to 'leadership';
- the essential task of co-creating far more innovative approaches to citizen participation and public problem solving.

I now provide a few remarks on each of these important features.

First, as explained in Chapter One, over the last forty years or so, globalization has weakened the power of place in the modern world, and this partly explains why societies have become so unequal. Fortunately, there is a counter-movement to place-less power. People care about the place where they live and they want to shape the quality of life in their community. We already know that the COVID-19 pandemic has prompted a remarkable escalation in place-based mutual aid and collaboration. This is a significant development and, as we look ahead, we need to build on this energizing resource. New Civic Leadership is explicitly committed to advancing the power of place-based communities and cities against the place-less power of external stakeholders who do not care about the spatial impacts of their decisions. New Civic Leadership starts, then, from a political understanding of power relations and recognizes that place represents a source of power.

Second, a problem with the use of the word 'public' to describe innovations in governance is that it may not excite the interest and enthusiasm of enlightened private sector actors. This is because 'public' is often seen as the opposite of 'private'.

The word 'civic' is more inclusive. Civic is closely related to the idea of the city or locality – to place, if you like. But it signals something more than place; it reminds actors of notions of civic virtue, conceived as a commitment by citizens to the common welfare of their communities. This is appealing to everyone who cares about the place where they live and work, whether they are employed in the public, private or non-profit sectors, or, indeed, if they are not in paid work.

Third, some writers have attempted to draw a sharp distinction between leadership and management. In an influential contribution, Warren Bennis and Burt Nanus suggested that: 'Managers do things right, and leaders do the right thing'.[27] This interpretation implies that managers focus on planning, managing and controlling, while leaders focus on the change-oriented process of visioning, networking, and building relationships.[28] This idea that managers strive for order and consistency, while leadership involves producing organizational change and movement can, however, be criticized for being too simplistic. As Nannerl Keohane explains: 'leaders are often engaged in managing or directing other people, and successful managers usually display some of the behaviours we identify with leadership, such as setting goals and mobilizing energies'.[29] However, as explained in Chapter One, successful leaders do more than manage processes and people. They listen to diverse views, put effort into coalition building, make an emotional connection, understand the value of experimentation, develop the collective intelligence of groups and organizations, and they change things. Above all, good civic leaders are adaptive and driven by moral purpose. In our post COVID-19 world, we certainly need talented managers, but the demand for high-quality civic leadership has sky-rocketed.

The fourth element of New Civic Leadership emphasizes innovation, not improvement. Improvement lies within the realm of traditional performance management. In public service organizations adopting an improvement strategy, politicians will, typically, set performance targets, require public servants to monitor inputs and outputs, assess outcomes and progress towards the targets, and then make adjustments to enhance service effectiveness.[30] By contrast, when an organization engages in innovation, it steps beyond conventional performance management. It undertakes a more radical assessment of its own effectiveness. When leaders strive for public service innovation, they recognize that the organization cannot deliver a significant increase in effectiveness by doing more of what it already knows how to do. We will return to this issue shortly.

The realms of place-based leadership

New Civic Leadership involves strong, place-based leadership acting to co-create new solutions to public problems, by drawing on the complementary strengths of civil society, the market and the state – see Figure 3.1 in Chapter Three. If we are to understand how effective, place-based leadership works, we need a conceptual framework that highlights the role of local leaders in facilitating collaboration and public service innovation.

Figure 4.2 suggests that in any given locality, place-based governance is likely to comprise five overlapping realms of place-based leadership, with leaders in each realm drawing on different sources of legitimacy:

- *political leadership* – referring to the work of those people elected to leadership positions by the citizenry;
- *public managerial/professional leadership* – referring to the work of public servants appointed by local authorities, governments and third sector organizations to plan and manage public services, and promote community wellbeing;
- *community leadership* – referring to the many civic-minded people who give their time and energy to local leadership activities in a wide variety of ways;

Figure 4.2: The realms of place-based leadership

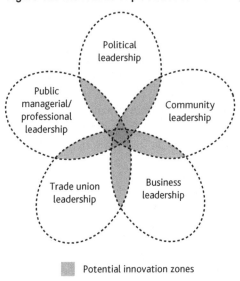

Potential innovation zones

Source: Hambleton R. (2015), p 127

- *business leadership* – referring to the contribution made by local business leaders and social entrepreneurs, who have a clear stake in the long-term prosperity of the locality;
- *trade union leadership* – referring to the efforts of trade union leaders striving to improve the pay and working conditions of employees.

These leadership roles are all important in cultivating and encouraging public service innovation and, crucially, they overlap. The areas of overlap can be described as innovation zones – areas providing many opportunities for inventive behaviour. This is because different perspectives are brought together in these zones and this can enable active questioning of established approaches.

It is fair to say that the areas of overlap shown in Figure 4.2 are often experienced as conflict zones, rather than innovation zones. These spaces do, of course, provide settings for power struggles between competing interests and values. Moreover, power is unequally distributed within these settings. This is precisely why place-based leadership matters. The evidence from my research on urban governance in different countries is that civic leadership is critical in ensuring that the innovation zones are orchestrated in a way that promotes a culture of listening that can, in turn, lead to co-creation and innovation. In Chapter Five, I offer Bristol as an example of inclusive civic leadership and, in Chapter Six, I provide some further examples of inspirational civic leadership.

In Chapter One, I introduced the topic of leadership and explained how the traditional top-down view is now widely recognized as being out of date. I explained how modern civic leaders, at least those who want to make a lasting difference, emphasize facilitative, or adaptive, approaches to leadership. In contrast to autocratic leaders, who stick to the top-down, 'I know best' approach, these enlightened modern leaders – and they are to be found in all of the five realms of civic leadership shown in Figure 4.2 – do not claim to have all the answers. Rather, they see their task as listening to diverse views in the other realms of leadership, putting significant efforts into coalition building and helping to co-develop the collective intelligence of groups and organizations. In an important sense, these leaders make an emotional connection to other participants and stakeholders in the governing process.

In Chapter Three, I suggested that our post COVID-19 world needs an unwavering commitment to progressive values. I suggested that a progressive, or inclusive, society is one in which 'all residents are able to participate fully in the society and the economy, and civic leaders strive for just results while caring for the natural environment on which we all depend'.[31] Civic leaders who share this progressive aim reach out to citizens and other stakeholders, and co-create ways of thinking and acting that step away from 'What's in it for me?' behaviour to embrace a 'How do we solve this problem together?' orientation. All kinds of people can contribute to New Civic Leadership and they may be inside or outside the state.

Having explained the five realms of place-based leadership, it is now possible to advance the presentation by engaging directly with the wider power struggles that cities and localities now face. In Chapter One, I set out some of the main reasons why place matters in the modern world. I also explained how place-less power is the chief obstacle lying in the path of those who want to advance the causes of social and economic justice, public health and environmental conservation in the modern world.

Put simply, enormously powerful place-less decision makers − located in the major multinational companies, banks and finance companies that now dominate the global economy − continue to take decisions *without* caring about the impacts of their decisions on communities living in particular places. This is morally wrong, economically unwise, socially destructive and environmentally disastrous. It follows that place-based leaders from all the realms of civic leadership shown in Figure 4.2 are, inevitably, faced with the challenge of facing down and negotiating with place-less power holders, to shift their perceptions and behaviour.

Figure 1.1 in Chapter One visualized the main constraints on place-based governance; Figure 4.3 locates the five realms of place-based leadership within this broader context. It is important to stress that, while the constraining forces are significant, the power of civic voice is well placed to expand local political space. If we take Europe as an example, as a matter of historical record, civic voices created elected local governments in many countries in the 19th century and early 20th century. Centralized state power was challenged and municipal authorities, answerable to local people, were created. We need a similar boldness of vision for the 21st century.

Place-based leadership: a danger zone to avoid

Before going further, I should provide a warning note about the power of place. Boosting the power of place should *not* be regarded as an unblemished panacea. Recall that it is very much

Figure 4.3: Place-based leadership in context

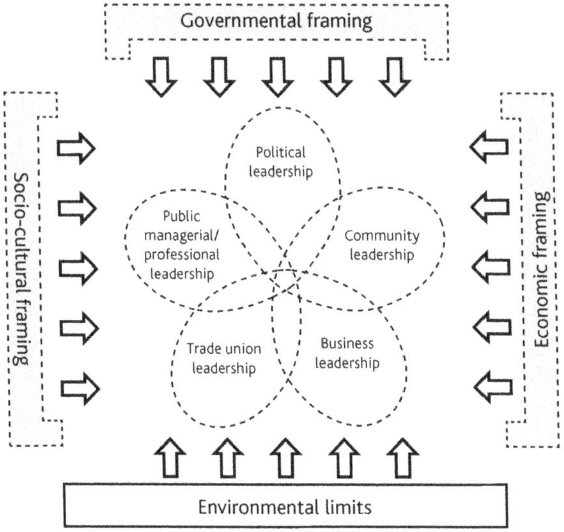

Source: Hambleton R. (2015), p 128

the case that, in the modern world, some geographical areas are formidably wealthy, whereas others experience grinding poverty and disadvantage. There is much fine scholarship documenting the existence of extreme territorial injustice in the modern world at different geographical scales – global, national and within cities and regions. For example, Carl Nightingale provides, in his book *Segregation: A global history of divided cities*, a magisterial analysis of the way we have managed to create astonishingly divided cities over the millennia.[32]

The growth of gated communities in cities highlights the concerns that Nightingale identifies in a rather striking way. Thirty years ago, Mike Davis was one of the first writers to recognize the threat that gated communities posed for the inclusive city. His prize-winning book on Los Angeles, *City of Quartz*, includes a chapter on 'Fortress LA', in which he records the insidious growth of walled communities. Never short of a vivid turn of phrase, he describes: '[a] frenzied ...

residential arms race as ordinary suburbanites demand the kind of social insulation once enjoyed only by the rich'.[33] It follows that some advocates of, for example, neighbourhood governance are interested in promoting socioeconomic divisions – in keeping rich neighbourhoods rich and, ideally, sealed off from other people.[34]

In this book, I am not seeking to promote this kind of selfish, parochial behaviour. Rather, following George Frederickson, distinguished professor of public administration at the University of Kansas, I am suggesting that place-based leaders should be guided by 'instincts of appropriateness' and by what is understood to be right and fair. Frederickson, as well as grasping the importance of facilitative leadership in the modern city, also makes a strong case for local leaders to transcend the geographical limitations of municipal boundaries: 'Although they are working from the vantage point of particular jurisdictions, leaders practising ... governance see the big social, economic and political context in which they are embedded ... To serve a city well, its leaders must transcend the city.'[35]

It follows that wise place-based leaders are not interested in 'beggar my neighbour' spatial competition. Rather, they are guided by a higher purpose, based on the progressive values that I outlined earlier.

Leading place-based collaborative governance

In the next chapter, I provide more details of a particular example of New Civic Leadership. At this point, however, it is helpful to identify three themes for post COVID-19 strategy that emerge from this chapter.

Progressive values

First, it is important to stress that values matter. As explained in Chapter Two, COVID-19 has drawn attention to the massive social and economic divides that now exist in many societies.

There has been an unacceptable growth in these inequalities in the last decade or two. The point has now been reached, where persistent inequality and unfairness threaten the stability of some Western democracies.

Outbreaks of public outrage and civil unrest, like those seen in the US following the death of George Floyd at the hands of police officers in Minneapolis on 25 May 2020, show that unequal cities and societies do not provide secure foundations for economic and social prosperity. The protests, skirmishes and street riots that took place in over 40 American cities in late May and early June 2020 drew attention to the existence of deep racial injustice in the country, but they reveal something more.

An effective response will need to go beyond radical reform of police policies and practices – deep-seated and structural inequalities will have to be addressed. Richard Wilson and Kate Pickett, in *The Spirit Level*, provide a helpful steer in this regard, showing that inequality is divisive and socially corrosive and that even those who are well off benefit from greater equality.[36]

In Chapter Three, I set out some ideas on the progressive values that civic leaders might want to consider as they develop their post COVID-19 recovery strategies. In essence, the suggestion made there is that market-driven ways of thinking can crowd out morals. If justice is to be advanced in the coming period, civic leaders will need to demonstrate an emotional commitment not just to tackling social and economic injustice, but also to caring for the natural environment on which we all depend.

Public innovation

A second important theme emerging from this chapter concerns public innovation. Figure 4.2 draws attention to the importance of creating innovation zones, meaning spaces that bring together leaders from the different realms of civic leadership shown in the diagram. The co-construction of these innovation zones is a key task for the collaborative leader. If these new spaces can be created and set up in the right way, unpredictable public innovation can be nurtured. Bring different kinds of people with different experiences into these spaces and, with the right kind of leadership, all kinds of things are possible.

Earlier in this chapter, I drew a distinction between improvement and innovation, and I build on that distinction here. In stable times, public service improvement strategies can suffice – performance targets can be set and progress can be monitored and assessed. To use the vocabulary put forward by Chris Argyris and Donald Schon in their influential book on organizational learning, this is single-loop learning (improvement, in my terms).[37] This kind of learning is rather like a thermostat. In more turbulent times, organizations need double-loop learning (innovation, in my terms). This occurs when concerns are detected that require modification of an organization's underlying norms and policies. Doing more of what is already known is not going to cut it. Frank Barrett, a professor of management and an accomplished musician, provides valuable insights from jazz on how to help organizations improvise.[38] In particular, Barrett shows that leaders need to embolden people to try something new, knowing that the results will, in all likelihood, be unexpected and 'unexpectable', including errors.[39]

Collaboration and partnership

A third theme to emerge is that collaboration and genuine partnership working will need to be given energetic attention. In Chapter Two, I suggested that COVID-19 lays down a peculiarly complex challenge to modern societies. It follows that the response needs to be equally complex.

Civic leaders, if they are able to draw on the strengths of the five realms of leadership shown in Figure 4.2, can use systems thinking to deliver suitably complex responses. The New Civic

Leadership framework provides pointers on how to co-create complex responses – meaning new ways of examining public challenges and coming up with more effective solutions. The literature on collaborative governance provides some helpful pointers on how to improve the quality of collaboration in cities and localities.[40]

A key insight from the literature is that, because collaborative leaders do not have formal power or authority to determine what different stakeholders do, they need to act as facilitative, not top-down, leaders, to use a distinction I drew in Chapter One. More than that, it follows that they need to develop their use of, what Joseph Nye describes as 'soft power'.[41] Soft power co-opts people, it wins them over. Successful collaborative leaders exercise strong leadership of the process: reaching out to different stakeholders, bringing in excluded voices, keeping participants actively engaged, celebrating successes, helping stakeholders to negotiate differences, and growing a culture of listening and respect that creates new possibilities.

Conclusions

In Chapter Three, I suggested that post COVID-19 recovery strategies will need to reconsider the dynamic interactions between the state, markets, civil society, nature and the individual. This chapter has attempted to extend our understanding of these interrelationships, by examining how the British welfare state came under pressure to change in the 1980s – see Figure 4.1. Alternative public service reform strategies have been considered and it has been shown that, following Albert Hirschman, there are two alternative ways of empowering people: by providing consumers with the power of exit; and by developing citizen voice. The introduction of simplistic private sector models into the public sector has been criticized and a New Civic Leadership approach – one that prizes citizen participation and civic virtue – has been put forward as a radical alternative to New Public Management.

New Civic Leadership is not a panacea, but it does have some merits. First, it comprehends the globalized power system that we all now live in. It recognizes the destructive social and environmental impact of place-less decision makers on the modern world, and it sets out to strengthen place-based power.

Second, it draws attention, following Jean-Jacques Rousseau, to the importance of civic activity, civic purpose and the cultivation of the civic imagination.

Third, New Civic Leadership provides practical insights for civic leaders on how to improve their approach to public leadership. It draws attention to:

- the importance of examining the external forces shaping the power of place and the need to consider how to expand local political space;
- the benefits of bringing together actors from the five realms of place-based leadership found in most localities, to engage in collaborative governance;
- the vital role of civic leadership in setting the tone for interactions and in orchestrating local processes of social discovery;
- the great benefits that can stem from setting up innovation zones, within which diverse actors can co-create new ideas and solutions.

In the next chapter, we will examine what happened when a British city decided to implement the New Civic Leadership approach.

Notes

[1] Jean-Jacques Rousseau (1762) *The Social Contract*, trans. Cranston M. (1968) *Rousseau: The Social Contract*, London: Penguin, Book III, Chapter 15, pp 140–141.

[2] Timmins N. (2001) *The Five Giants: A biography of the welfare state* (2nd edn), London: Harper Collins; Titmuss R. (2019) *Essays on the Welfare State*, Bristol: Policy Press (first published 1958 by George Allen and Unwin Ltd).

[3] These remarks draw on: Burns D., Hambleton R. and Hoggett P. (1994) *The Politics of Decentralisation: Revitalising local democracy*, Basingstoke: Palgrave, pp 21–27.

[4] Burns D., Hambleton R. and Hoggett P. (1994 p 22) (see Note 3).

[5] See, for example: Taylor M. (2011) *Public Policy in the Community* (2nd edn), Basingstoke: Palgrave; Oliver B. and Pitt B. (2013) *Engaging Communities and Service Users: Context, themes and methods*, Basingstoke: Palgrave.

[6] In some countries, for example in Germany and the Netherlands, the third sector has played an important role in welfare services since the Second World War.

[7] Brandsen T. and Pestoff V. (2006) 'Co-production, the third sector and the delivery of public services', *Public Management Review*, 8(4): 493–501; Sicilia M., Sancino A., Nabatchi T. and Guarini E. (2019) 'Facilitating co-production in public services: Management implications from a systematic literature review', *Public Money and Management*, 39(4): 233–240.

[8] See, for example: Osborne D. and Plastrik P. (1997) *Banishing Bureaucracy*, Reading, MA: Addison-Wesley; Smith S. and Milligan A. (2015) *On Purpose: Delivering a branded customer experience people love*, London: Kogan Page.

[9] Hirschman A.O. (1970) *Exit, Voice and Loyalty*, Cambridge, MA: Harvard University Press.

[10] It is worth noting that major private sector companies have, in a stealthy and largely unnoticed way, expanded not just their knowledge of customers but also their ability to influence them. See: Zuboff S. (2019) *The Age of Surveillance Capitalism: Fighting for the future at the new frontier of power*, London: Profile Books Ltd.

[11] Locality (2020) *We Were Built For This: How community organisations helped us through the coronavirus crisis – and how we can build a better future*, June, London: Locality. More information at: https://locality.org.uk/policy-campaigns/leading-the-coronavirus-recovery/

[12] The social enterprise was wound up in 2015, but it has a useful legacy website: www.participle.net

[13] Hambleton R. and Howard J. (2012) *Public Sector Innovation and Local Leadership in the UK and The Netherlands*, York: Joseph Rowntree Foundation. In this action research project, we linked the Swindon team with a team in the Netherlands who were using another novel approach to welfare reform, known as the Social GP model.

[14] For more information on this way of thinking, see: Cottam H. (2018) *Radical Help: How we can remake the relationships between us and revolutionise the welfare state*, London: Virago.

[15] Wainwright H. (2003) *Reclaim the State: Experiments in popular democracy*, London: Verso.

[16] Smith G. (2009) *Democratic Innovations: Designing institutions for citizen participation*, Cambridge: Cambridge University Press; Rocke A. (2014) *Framing Citizen Participation: Participatory budgeting in France, Germany and the United Kingdom*, Basingstoke: Palgrave. The PB network, based in the UK, advocates for learning and innovation in participatory budgeting: https://pbnetwork.org.uk

[17] The details of how to organize citizens' assemblies vary. A useful resource outlining principles, models and methods is provided by the UK charity *Involve*: https://www.involve.org.uk

[18] For more information, see: https://www.citizensassembly.ie/en/

[19] For more information, see: https://rebellion.earth/act-now/resources/citizens-assembly/

[20] The term first appeared in academic circles in 1991: Hood C. (1991) 'A public management for all seasons?', *Public Administration*, 69(1): 3–19; Hoggett P. (1991) 'A new management in the public sector?', *Policy and Politics*, 19(4): 243–256.

[21] Ferlie E., Ashburner L., Fitzgerald L. and Pettigrew A. (1996) *The New Public Management in Action*, Oxford: Oxford University Press; Lane J.E. (2000) *New Public Management*, London: Routledge.

[22] See, for example: Whitfield D. (2001) *Public Services or Corporate Welfare*, London: Pluto Press; Whitfield D. (2020) *Public Alternative to the Privatisation of Life*, Nottingham: Spokesman.

[23] Mintzberg H. (1996) 'Managing government. Governing management', *Harvard Business Review*, May-June, 75–83.

[24] See, for example: Osborne S.P. (ed) (2010) *The New Public Governance? Emerging perspectives on the theory and practice of public governance*, Abingdon: Routledge; Benington J. and Moore M.H. (eds) (2011) *Public Value: Theory and practice*, Basingstoke: Palgrave; Bovaird T. and Loeffler E. (eds) (2015) *Public Management and Governance*, Abingdon: Routledge; Bryson J. M., Crosby B.C. and Bloomberg L. (eds) (2015) *Public Value and Public Administration*, Washington DC: Georgetown Press; Brandsen T., Steen T. and Verschuere B. (eds) (2018) *Co-production and Co-creation: Engaging citizens in public services*, Abingdon: Routledge; and Pestoff V. (2019) *Co-production and Public Service Management: Citizenship, governance and public services management*, Abingdon: Routledge.

[25] Fung A. (2004) *Empowered Participation: Reinventing urban democracy*, Princeton, NJ: Princeton University Press; Majoor S., Morel M., Straathof A., Suurenbroek F. and van Wilden W. (2017) *Lab Amsterdam: Working, learning, reflections*, Amsterdam: Amsterdam University of Applied Sciences; Hertting N. and Kugelberg C. (eds) (2018) *Local Participatory Governance and Representative Democracy in European Cities*, Abingdon: Routledge; and Heinelt H. (ed) (2018) *Handbook on Participatory Governance*, Cheltenham: Edward Elgar.

[26] Fuller details of the New Civic Leadership framework are set out in: Hambleton R. (2015) *Leading the Inclusive City: Place-based innovation for a bounded planet*, Bristol: Policy Press, pp 115–132.

[27] Bennis W.G. and Nanus B. (1985) *Leaders: Strategies for taking charge*, New York: Harper Collins, p 21.

[28] See Kotter J.P. (1988) *The Leadership Factor*, New York: Free Press.

[29] Keohane N.O. (2010) *Thinking About Leadership*, Princeton, NJ: Princeton University Press, p 37.

[30] This idea of performance management, or performance planning, remains a dominant model in public management. See, for example: Joyce P. (2012) *Strategic Leadership in Public Services*, Abingdon: Routledge; Ashdown L. (2018) *Performance Management: A practical introduction*, London: Chartered Institute of Personnel and Development.

[31] Hambleton (2015 p 25) (see Note 26).

[32] Nightingale C.H. (2012) *Segregation: A global history of divided cities*, Chicago: The University of Chicago Press.

[33] Davis M. (1990) *City of Quartz: Excavating the future of Los Angeles*, London: Verso, p 246.

[34] For more details, see Hambleton (2015 pp 102–106) (see Note 26).

[35] Frederickson H.G. (2005) 'Transcending the community: Local leadership in a world of shared power', *Public Management*, 87, p 10.

[36] Wilkinson R. and Pickett K. (2010) *The Spirit Level: Why equality is better for everyone*, London: Penguin.

[37] Argyris C. and Schon D.A. (1978) *Organizational Learning: A theory of action perspective*, Reading, MA: Addison-Wesley.

[38] Barrett F.J. (2012) *Yes to the Mess: Surprising leadership lessons from jazz*, Boston, MA: Harvard Business Review Press.

[39] This discussion of public innovation is curtailed. For a more extended discussion, see Hambleton (2015 pp 139–171) (Note 26).

[40] Ansell C. and Gash A. (2008) 'Collaborative governance in theory and practice', *Journal of Public Administration Research and Theory*, 18(4): 543–571; Page S. (2010) 'Integrative leadership for collaborative governance: Civic engagement in Seattle', *The Leadership Quarterly*, 21(2): 246–263; Williams P. (2012) *Collaboration in Public Policy and Practice: Perspectives on boundary spanners*, Bristol: Policy Press; Ansell C. and Torfing J. (eds) (2014) *Public Innovation Through Collaboration and Design*, Abingdon: Routledge.

[41] Nye J.S. (2004) *Soft Power: The means of success in world politics*, New York: Public Affairs.

FIVE

The Bristol One City Approach

Introduction

Marvin Rees began to develop the idea of creating a Bristol City Office in the summer of 2015. At the time, he was competing to be selected as the Labour Party candidate to run for Mayor of Bristol in the May 2016 local election. In the simplest of terms, his City Office concept represents an attempt to unite public purpose in the city. It seeks to bind together all those who care about the city in a much more effective collaborative effort. The approach is strongly place-based, in the sense that it draws inspiration and enthusiasm from the positive feelings that people have about the place where they live.

In a headline on his campaign website in August 2015, Rees signalled the nature of the shift that he had in mind: 'Bristol shouldn't be run from the council chamber'. This, in itself, was a radical statement for a politician seeking public office. In various speeches he explained that, while elected local government is enormously important in city governance, it is the way that public organizations work in creative collaboration with other interests in the city that holds out real promise for making social, economic and environmental progress.

In the autumn of 2015, shortly after he was selected as the Labour Party candidate for mayor, I had my first detailed conversation with Marvin about city governance. He had read my book on *Leading the Inclusive City* and we discussed ways of putting his City Office idea into effect.[1] Marvin found the concept of realms of civic leadership to be particularly helpful – see Figure 4.2. He told me that he saw this figure as a 'flower diagram' and that the City Office should be located at the heart of this growing flower. In his mind, the City Office needed to draw insight and energy from all the five realms of place-based leadership shown in the diagram.

In the May 2016 mayoral election, Rees, and the Labour Party, won a resounding victory. Rees attracted the votes of 68,750 citizens, a figure that was over 29,000 more than the incumbent mayor, George Ferguson, an independent politician. The local election also saw the election of 37 Labour Party councillors, and this gave the Labour Party a majority of four on the 70-seat city council. The mayor and all councillors were elected for a four-year term.[2] The stage was set for a radical shift towards a much more collaborative approach to urban governance in Bristol.

This chapter provides an account of the steps taken, starting in 2016, to deliver what became known as: the Bristol One City Approach. It records how one city attempted to improve urban governance by using the New Civic Leadership concepts and ideas set out in the previous chapter. An opening section provides a brief orientation to the City of Bristol, its history, culture and politics. Bristol is a prosperous city, but it also has significant social, economic and racial divisions. The One City Approach was designed to tackle these persistent inequalities. In 2012, the citizens of Bristol decided in a referendum to introduce a new city governance system, one that would be headed by a directly elected mayor, and this new system is explained. The heart of this chapter provides an outline of the main elements of the Bristol One City Approach. The claim will be made that, because civic leaders in Bristol transformed their working relationships in the 2016–19 period, they were much better placed to respond creatively to the COVID-19 onslaught when it arrived.

Bristol: historic, vibrant, divided

Bristol is a vibrant city with a rich heritage, a lively arts scene and an established reputation for innovation within the creative and high-tech industrial sectors. In 2017, *The Sunday Times* rated Bristol the best place to live in Britain, describing it as 'a small city that feels like a big city' and stating with perhaps too much enthusiasm: 'We sum the city up as cool, classy and supremely creative'.[3] When this news came out, the Mayor of Bristol, Marvin Rees, said: 'Pinpointing what makes Bristol special isn't easy. It's a combination of many things from the people to the place itself, but at the heart of it is our cultural diversity and independent spirit.'

It is noteworthy that residents of the city (population: 463,000) speak over 90 languages. The city contains over 4,000 heritage, or 'listed', buildings and has a number of famous historic destinations that make the city attractive to tourists, notably the Clifton Suspension Bridge and the SS Great Britain. The city is, then, both multicultural and prosperous and, according to a range of traditional economic indicators, for example employment levels and GDP per head, it compares very well with other provincial cities in the UK.

History tells us that Bristol's rise in prosperity was linked to its port, especially to the importation of tobacco and wine and to its active participation in the slave trade.[4] Bristol's involvement in the slave trade was, in fact, substantial. Historian Kenneth Morgan indicates that, in the late 17th century: 'Bristol pulled ahead of London, its main early rival in the slave trade, only to be overtaken by Liverpool in the 1740s'.[5] We will come back to Bristol's involvement in the slave trade in a moment.

Despite the relative economic success of the city, the evidence shows that Bristol has become, to use Charles Dickens' famous phrase, 'a tale of two cities'. It is troubling to record that social and economic inequality within the city has grown in the period since 2010. A study carried out by Bristol City Council in 2019 found that Bristol has some of the most deprived areas in the country, sitting right next to some of the least deprived areas in the country.[6] Some 15 per cent of Bristol residents (70,000 people) live in the most deprived 10 per cent of areas in England. Given these shocking statistics, it is not surprising that life expectancy within Bristol also varies dramatically. In 2019, the gap in life expectancy between the most deprived and the least deprived groups in Bristol was 9.6 years for men and 7.1 years for women.[7] Marvin Rees drew attention to these disparities when he campaigned to become Mayor of Bristol in 2016, and he has promoted efforts to address them in his One City Approach to city leadership.

Bristol and the Black Lives Matter movement

On 7 June 2020, Black Lives Matter protesters in Bristol pulled down a statue of the prolific slave trader Edward Colston, hauled it along the ground and, to the cheers of onlookers, dumped it into Bristol Harbour. The photograph of the bronze statue of the slave trader splashing into the water had a global impact. That day, Bristol was only one of thousands of cities and communities across the world protesting against the killing of George Floyd by American police officers in Minneapolis, Minnesota, on 25 May 2020. As mentioned in Chapter Two, Floyd, a 46-year-old black man, died while being arrested by four police officers despite the distressed man crying out 'I can't breathe'.

There are many reasons why the civil disobedience in Bristol resonated so powerfully with such an extensive and diverse global audience. Three can be highlighted. First, Edward Colston (1636–1721), a prolific slave trader and Tory Member of Parliament, had a thoroughly appalling record. Colston was an influential member of the Royal African Company, which held a monopoly on trading along the west coast of Africa. It is estimated that his company was involved in the transportation of 84,000 men, women and children from Africa to be sold as slaves in the Caribbean and elsewhere in the Americas. Of them, it is believed that 19,000 died in the middle passage on the journey from Africa to the plantations in the New World. The splash of Colston's statue, as it entered the harbour, recalled the way in which innocent Africans were cast into the sea as the slave ships crossed the Atlantic.

Second, the removal of the statue spoke to the heart of the Black Lives Matter movement. Here was a vivid symbol of brutal oppression by established power over black people that should have been removed from the public realm decades ago.

Third, the policing of the event by Avon and Somerset Police was exceptionally good – it was empathetic, wise and proportionate. Andy Bennett, the Bristol Area Commander in charge of policing on the day, explained that thousands of demonstrators had protested peacefully and his actions were designed to keep people safe. On 8 June 2020, Andy Marsh, Chief Constable of Avon and Somerset Police, backed up his superintendent: 'I fully support the actions of my officers, they responded with common sense, sound judgement and in the best interest of public safety'.[8] This sophisticated and skilful approach to policing, one designed to protect people from injury and suffering, can be contrasted with the militaristic, brute force, 'dominate the streets' approach deployed by US President Donald Trump in his response to the many similar public protests in the US. It is not difficult to ascertain which approach to policing is likely to be more successful in maintaining peace, building understanding and enhancing the problem-solving capacity of cities and communities.

Marvin Rees, Mayor of Bristol, said: 'I do not condone criminal damage … At the same time … I'm a descendant of Jamaicans… and I can't say that that statue was anything other than offensive to me …'[9] At the time of writing, Bristol City Council is considering placing the damaged statue in a city museum, together with the many messages left on placards by the Black Lives Matter protesters at the base of the plinth on which the bronze statue had once stood. In this way, the toppling of the slave trader's statue can, perhaps, become an important part of the history of Bristol.

This short description of the Black Lives Matter protests in Bristol in the early summer of 2020 shows that the Bristol One City Approach, launched in 2016, was on the right track. As Mayor Rees explained, in an interview with the UK *Local Government Chronicle* in July 2020, the city was already actively working to overcome inequality and the downing of the statue gave a 'sense of urgency' to this task. He explained that the challenge facing the city is not just about race, it's about race and class and the focus needs to be on tackling social immobility:

'When we really manage to crack the challenge of social immobility then that will be dealing with racism because racism is about confining you to the socioeconomic status of your parents who were disadvantaged because of the colour of their skin, but you also unlock opportunities for working class and white poor people too.'[10]

We will return to the theme of tackling inequality shortly.

The introduction of mayoral governance in Bristol

Let's step back a little and look at the way the governance of Bristol has evolved in the last ten years or so. As mentioned earlier, the citizens of Bristol, in a referendum held in May 2012, decided to introduce a mayoral form of governance. Our touch on this subject can be light, as the reasons why this shift took place and the initial impacts are documented in some detail elsewhere.[11] While the directly elected mayor model of governance is well established in many countries, it is still relatively new to the UK. As David Sweeting has explained, the three linked features of this model of governance are: direct election of the political leader of the city by the citizens; an election process that creates a single, identifiable city leader;

and an election process that delivers a secure term of office for the city leader.[12]

The UK Localism Act 2011 required the 12 largest cities in England to hold referendums, to decide whether or not to adopt a directly elected mayor model of governance. In the event, ten referendums were held in May 2012 as two cities – Liverpool and Salford – opted to introduce a mayoral model using existing legislation. In nine cities, local citizens rejected the mayoral form of governance; Bristol was the only city to vote 'yes'.

The reasons why Bristol citizens bucked the national trend and voted for radical change are complex. Some voters felt that the perceived short-termism of political parties was holding Bristol back, and that there was an urgent need for more stability in city leadership. Others felt that Bristol was not 'punching its weight' in national and international circles. It is also the case that the 'Vote Yes' campaign was remarkably well organized and very effective in advocating the case for governance reform.

The subsequent election, held in November 2012, attracted 15 mayoral candidates, more than in any other mayoral election in England. George Ferguson, an independent candidate, caused a national stir by beating all the established political parties. Ferguson, an architect and urbanist, noted for always wearing red trousers, was able to use his long experience of bringing about successful regeneration projects in the city to his electoral advantage. In office, Mayor Ferguson promoted an external-facing style of leadership. The international reputation of the city received a significant boost, when Bristol was recognized by the European Union as European Green Capital in 2015. Ferguson always maintained that the groundwork for this achievement was carried out before he was elected, but it is clear that he deserves credit for bringing his own personal enthusiasm and commitment to this initiative.

Reflecting his interests and priorities, Ferguson delivered a number of important environmental shifts in public policy during his tenure. For example, he took bold steps to improve safety on the streets and to modify travel behaviour in the city. A speed limit of 20 miles per hour was introduced across virtually the entire city, and there was a rapid expansion of Resident Parking Zones (RPZs) in neighbourhoods circling the city centre. This policy removed free parking spaces, previously available to commuters who used to drive into these neighbourhoods and then walk to work in the city centre. RPZs require residents to buy parking permits so that they can park locally. The measures were not popular with everyone, but they delivered significant environmental and public safety benefits.

A downside of Mayor Ferguson's leadership was that it was top-down in style, and arrangements for civic participation in decision making were felt to be relatively weak. It is also the case that tackling the ingrained inequality in the city, mentioned earlier, did not receive the attention it warranted.[13]

Marvin Rees, Mayor of Bristol since 2016

Born in 1972, Marvin Rees is mixed-race and has a working-class background. Father of three, he is the son of an English mother and a Jamaican father. In his early life, he went through tough times, at one point living in a Women's Refuge with his mother. He was brought up by his mother, living at various times, in St Paul's, Laurence Weston and Easton, all relatively deprived neighbourhoods within Bristol. He is rooted in the community and social networks of St Paul's and has a long history of civic activism, notably in relation to youth work. Rees ran for mayor in 2012 and lost to George Ferguson by 6,094 votes. This was a massive personal and political setback. In a documentary film made about his election campaigns in both 2012 and 2016, he expressed his feelings openly. Shortly after his 2012 defeat, he expressed doubts about whether he would be able to continue in politics.[14]

Rees showed great personal courage in overcoming the setback of his mayoral defeat in 2012. As mentioned earlier, he ran for office again and became Bristol's second directly elected mayor in May 2016. He was 45 years old and became the first-ever directly elected mayor of black African-Caribbean descent to lead any European city. A young and charismatic black man, an individual who is directly descended from people who were enslaved, became the democratically elected leader of a city that had been a major player in the transatlantic slave trade. This, by any standards, was an extraordinary achievement.

In Chapter One I contrasted two styles of leadership. Put simply, top-down leaders claim to know the answers and they issue guidance or, more often than not, instructions to their subordinates. In American urban political science this is often described as the 'city boss' model of leadership.[15] In contrast, facilitative leadership emphasizes the importance of listening to the views of others and putting serious effort into learning and coalition building. Mayor Rees demonstrated his strong commitment to the latter approach on his first day in office.

A few days after being elected, Rees, at his swearing-in ceremony on 9 May 2016 in the M-Shed, a museum documenting the history of the people of Bristol, showed that he wanted to develop a collective, not an individualized, approach to city leadership. Note that this ceremony was not held in City Hall, as was the tradition. Rather, this important civic event was located in a public building in the centre of the city that is visited by large numbers of Bristol residents. The symbolism was clear – City Hall is only part of the governance of the city.

Most unusually for a swearing-in ceremony, the Mayor was not the only speaker on the platform offering ideas on the future of the city. After the formal swearing-in procedure, Rees introduced Miles Chambers, later to become the first Bristol Poet Laureate, who read a passionate poem about the history of the city. Rees then invited three other civic leaders in Bristol to offer their ideas for the future of the city: a senior health services manager; the Vice-Chancellor of one of the two local universities; and the Bristol Area Commander of Avon and Somerset Police. Rees did not know in advance what these civic leaders were going to say. From the get-go, then, Rees was signalling his interest in sharing power and valuing the leadership contributions of other agencies and actors. In his own speech, Rees emphasized that the City Office model of city leadership, a notion he had spelt out in his campaign for mayor, was intended to improve partnership working and would emphasize the co-creation of new ideas and ways of working.

The Bristol One City Approach

In Chapter Two, I drew attention to the complexity of the challenges laid down by the COVID-19 pandemic. A key point emerging from that discussion is that complex challenges require an equally complex response.[16] The Bristol One City Approach provides an example of how one city is attempting to respond to the complexity of modern public policy challenges by developing an array of responses. It must be said that this place-based approach to problem solving has been severely hindered by the super-centralization of power within central government in the UK.[17] The central state has held Bristol back. In Chapter Seven, we will return to this topic and explore the importance of strengthening the power of elected local authorities across the world, in order to enable them to respond creatively to unforeseen developments.

Here, however, we can note that, notwithstanding the absence of significant fiscal place-based power within Bristol City Council, civic leaders have made impressive progress in developing a new approach to collaborative governance. If we go straight to the present, we can state that the City of Bristol now has an agreed One City Plan for the next thirty years and, more important, this plan is underpinned by a One City Approach, which brings together actors from the different realms of civic leadership, outlined in the last chapter, in an active process of social discovery and decision making.

This means that all the major players in the city are not just signed up to the aim of delivering a fair, healthy, sustainable and inclusive city, but they also serve on a City Leaders Group that meets regularly to ensure that this vision is actually delivered. Six thematic boards, bringing together a diversity of voices, are now working to support the City Leaders Group in ensuring that the ambitious goals agreed in the One City Plan come to fruition. These steps to build new, collaborative governance structures are underpinned by the efforts of a very small, but extraordinarily able, City Office team that works to orchestrate a remarkable amount of cross-sector collaboration and problem solving.[18]

But I am jumping ahead. How did this new, collaborative governance infrastructure come to be co-created? We can summarize the Bristol governance innovation story by referring to four themes:

- beyond partnership working;
- co-creating a One City Plan;
- boosting place-based leadership talent;
- developing the collective intelligence of the city.

Beyond partnership working: co-creating solutions

As mentioned earlier, the City Office aims to mobilize energies from all five realms of place-based leadership (see Figure 4.2) for the benefit of the whole city. These realms are: political leadership; public managerial/professional leadership; community leadership; business leadership; and trade union leadership. The overlaps between these realms can, with the right kind of overall civic leadership, become powerful innovation zones – spaces within which actors can co-create new ways of thinking and new solutions.

The central ethos is to focus on making an *additional* contribution over and above the activities of existing agencies and established collaborative arrangements. The City Office strives to add value by accessing networks and resources that otherwise would not be available. It does this by creating innovation zones, by developing collaborative projects and by building new cross-sector relationships via City Gatherings.

From the outset, Rees wanted to create a programme of inclusive City Gatherings of civic leaders, the idea being to draw together leaders from *all* the five realms of place-based leadership on a regular basis. On 23 July 2016, the first City Gathering was held at We The Curious, a public-friendly centre for science exploration located in the heart of Bristol. City Gatherings, which now take place every six months or so, are not conventional public meetings. Rather, they are designed to create highly interactive city conversations, with participants working together in cross-cutting teams, to examine the major challenges facing the city and to explore ideas on how to tackle them.

The first City Gathering was expected to bring together around 30 civic leaders. In the event, the location had to be changed to a bigger venue, as over 70 civic leaders wanted to participate. The ninth City Gathering, held on 10 January 2020, attracted over 300 civic leaders. The tenth City Gathering, held virtually on 26 June 2020, which had 270 participants, included contributions from Vivienne Faull, the Bishop of Bristol, David Olusoga, the influential historian who has reshaped our understanding of the role of black people in British history, and Lord Kerslake, who is leading the UK2070 Commission.

The City Gatherings, in and of themselves, represent an extraordinary expansion of civic engagement and commitment to public problem solving. City Gatherings have developed a remarkably influential role in stimulating the co-creation of new ideas, in identifying issues for priority attention and in building social networks and civic capacity. It needs to be stressed that the City Gatherings are nothing like the conventional partnership working arrangements that used to exist in the city in the past.

Helping people from the different realms of leadership to make new connections is critical, and there are different ways of doing this. Shortly after being elected, Rees created an innovation zone in City Hall, just outside the Mayor's Office. People, from any of the realms of civic leadership shown in Figure 4.2, who are working on activities relating to the City Office agenda, are invited to work in this open-plan office space on Tuesdays. In addition, the City Office organizes occasional presentations and workshops on Tuesday mornings. The creation of this physical space, clearly an innovation zone within the New Civic Leadership model of co-governance outlined in Chapter Four, is a simple, cost-free step that enables informal relationship building to flourish.

The City Office has promoted and supported a large number of imaginative projects bringing together actors from the five realms of civic leadership. The issues for attention stem from the recommendations of the City Gatherings mentioned earlier. There are far too many City Office initiatives to list in this short account, but to illustrate the approach here are three examples:

• *The Street Homelessness Challenge project*. Arising from concerns expressed at the first City Gathering, in late 2016, Rees asked local leaders from the five realms of civic leadership to work together to create 100 extra beds for homeless people in the first 100 days of 2017. A project group, chaired by the City Office director, was set up to develop ways of achieving this ambitious target. City Office partners launched a 'spectrum of activity' to tackle homelessness.[19] This inclusive approach brought in actors not normally involved in addressing homelessness – for example local businesses, including the local bus company. The initiative delivered 34 new bed-spaces within the 100 days, as well as arrangements to deliver two double-decker buses to provide 20 additional emergency bed-spaces. The collaborative work did not meet the ambitious target, but extra bed-spaces were added and new working relationships were created.

- *The Feeding Bristol Healthy Holiday programme.* The City Gathering held in January 2019 expressed concern about food insecurity in the city and, in particular, the worrying fact that children from poor families do not receive free school meals during holidays. In spring 2019, when anticipated funding from UK central government for a Feeding Bristol Healthy Holiday 2019 programme did not materialize, Feeding Bristol, a civic initiative that gained charity status in 2018, launched a community-based effort to raise funds. This initiative, which was supported by the City Office, raised £125,000 from over fifty organizations in a matter of weeks. The collaborative model developed by Mayor Rees was critical in helping Feeding Bristol to deliver over 50,000 meals, provided by over 120 organizations, to 5,000 needy children, over the six-week summer period in 2019.[20]

- *The Period Friendly Bristol initiative.* The January 2019 City Gathering also identified an injustice that many didn't know existed in Bristol. Many women and girls were being denied period dignity, with little or no access to menstrual products. The City Gathering decided that a new collaborative initiative to tackle period poverty should be one of the top three priorities in 2019 for the new Bristol One City Plan. Led by Councillor Helen Godwin, Cabinet Lead for Women, Children and Families, this initiative has brought many new voices into the discussion, including the experiences of young people. Key achievements so far have been: a major effort to address period stigma through education, including the production of a film presenting the views of teenage girls and boys that is now being used in schools across Bristol and more widely; and the development of a city-wide donation and distribution network of free sanitary products, with a pilot effort launched in 2020 to distribute products to community centres, GP surgeries, leisure centres and libraries in priority neighbourhoods.[21]

Co-creating a Bristol One City Plan and City Fund

A very important achievement of the Bristol City Office is not just the co-creation of the first Bristol One City Plan, but also the securing of civic commitment to delivering it. The idea of developing a shared long-term vision for the future trajectory of the city emerged from discussions at several of the early City Gatherings. It became the focus of attention at the fifth City Gathering, held in the conference facility at Ashton Gate, the home of Bristol City Football Club in December 2017. This highly interactive session developed a collective understanding of the main issues that needed to be addressed, and cross-sector teams were set up to take the initiative forward.

The Bristol One City Plan was launched at a City Gathering in January 2019. This ambitious plan is designed to orchestrate the creation of a 'big picture' strategy for the future development of the city – one that looks forward to 2050, and one that agencies are expected to commit to.[22] The central aim is to create a city that is fair, healthy and sustainable. It is important to emphasize that this is *not* a conventional city council plan – it is a collective plan that sees the city council's activities as part of a much broader civic effort. As mentioned earlier, it is a plan that enjoys the public support of a Bristol City Leaders Group – a group representing leaders from the five realms of civic leadership shown in Figure 4.2. The plan is reviewed on an annual basis and is rolled forward each January.

Additionally, it is important to highlight two novel features of the Bristol One City Plan. First, Bristol is one of a relatively small number of cities to take meticulous account of the Sustainable Development Goals (SDGs) agreed by every country in the world in 2015.[23] The SDGs set out 17 goals and 169 targets in a blueprint to achieve a better and more sustainable future for all by 2030. As part of the preparation of the One City Plan, Bristol conducted what is known as a Voluntary Local Review, which is, basically, an assessment of how well the city is doing on delivering the SDGs. David Donoghue, former Irish Ambassador to the United Nations, who co-negotiated the agreement on the SDGs with 193 member states, participated in the Bristol City Gathering in January 2020 and stated that:

'Bristol is a shining light nationally and internationally as somewhere that has been taking meaningful action on the UN Sustainable Development Goals. Cities will need to meet the SDG agenda and Bristol is at the forefront.'[24]

Second, the City Office has co-created a new way of funding delivery of priority elements set out in the One City Plan. Established in April 2018, the City Funds Board, which brings together representatives from communities, business, finance, the public sector and the two local universities, is developing new match-funding initiatives to focus finance via repayable loans and grant giving, on the priority areas set out in the Bristol One City Plan.[25] The 2020 fund, worth £10 million, has focused on economic inclusion, community initiatives, child hunger and moving Bristol towards being a carbon-neutral city.

Boosting place-based leadership talent

The third element in the One City Approach is the development of place-based leadership talent. The City Gatherings identified the importance of developing and delivering new kinds of civic leadership programmes, ones that target underrepresented groups in the city. The City Office was encouraged to orchestrate a step-change in the provision of place-based leadership opportunities – ranging from city leadership courses for young people (under 19s) through to advanced place-based leadership workshops for rising leaders from the realms of leadership shown in Figure 4.2.[26]

Stepping Up, a city-wide, award-winning leadership programme, provides an example. Launched in 2017, Stepping Up is designed to encourage and support black and minority ethnic groups, and other groups that have been held back by discrimination, to progress in their careers. The aim is to make the leadership of the public, commercial and voluntary sectors in Bristol much more diverse. Councillor Asher Craig, Deputy Mayor of Bristol, has taken a lead on developing this new programme. Interviewed in January 2020, she said:

'When we started out we imagined having 25 people in the programme. The first annual round was 57, there are 47 on it this year, including a good number of Somali women. Now over 60 organisations in this city are engaged in the Stepping Up initiative ... And a massive number of mentoring hours are now being put in for free by the many people who support this initiative ... This is a great example of One City working.'[27]

The Stepping Up programme has already been nominated for a national local government award for promoting diversity and inclusion.[28]

Developing the collective intelligence of the city

Bristol has two universities – the University of Bristol and the University of the West of England, Bristol – and they have both been actively involved in helping to develop the Bristol One City Approach. In the US, most universities, particularly the public universities, have understood the value of engaged scholarship for over 150 years.[29] The American public university has, from the outset, aimed to fuse scholarly inspiration with a strong commitment to practical application. This value stance has advanced the quality of American scholarship, while also benefiting the cities where these universities are located.[30] By comparison, British universities have, until recently, tended to be relatively detached from their surroundings. They have not, on the whole, been very active contributors to public problem solving in the places where they are located – so much so that I was moved to ask whether some of them could be described as the 'sleeping giants of place-based leadership'.[31]

Well before he was elected in 2016, Mayor Rees recognized that the two local universities could make a major contribution to the work of his new City Office. In 2017, he invited me to explore possibilities with both universities for advancing academic engagement with the City Office and, in early 2018, a small team, bringing together colleagues from the two universities and the City Office, started to meet on a regular basis.[32] We drew inspiration from the work of the Atlanta Studies Network, a grouping that links scholars at several universities in Atlanta with a variety of civic agencies in the city.[33] The network organizes an annual symposium, at which scholars studying Atlanta can share insights and research findings with a view to, among other things, improving public policy making in Atlanta.[34]

We developed our own version of this approach, one that is linked directly to the Bristol One City Plan, and the first Bristol Forum was held in March 2019.[35] This one-day, 'free to attend' event brought together over 200 participants from across academia, business, the third sector and the public sector to explore the challenges facing the city and the city region, and to develop potential solutions. Over 70 presentations and interactive discussions took place, new relationships were established and various projects were initiated. A key strength of the Bristol Forum is that it brings different perspectives into the conversation about how to develop, deliver and update the Bristol One City Plan. By way of national context, it is encouraging to note that, following the publication of an influential report by the independent Civic University Commission in 2019, a significant number of British universities have taken steps to elevate their civic engagement efforts.[36] The many and varied steps taken by the two universities in Bristol are in line with the aims and objectives of the new Civic University Network.[37]

The Bristol response to COVID-19

The One City response to the COVID-19 emergency has many components, too many to cover adequately here. Fortunately, there is more detail on the Bristol One City website for those who wish to follow up.[38] Bristol City Council, working with One City partners, developed a sophisticated communications strategy at a very early stage. In April 2020 an unmissable, broad yellow band was introduced across the top of the home page of the City Council website, with the heading 'Coronavirus (COVID-19): Service updates and health advice'. Click on this band and you were presented with clear and well-organized information and advice on 'What you need to know' under nine headings: Government and NHS advice; Changes to services; Get help; Help others; Businesses; NHS and key workers; Contact us; Accessible information; and Video update from the Mayor. Click through on any one of these to find more detailed information and, of course, more click-through options were provided, to enable the user to drill down with great ease.

While there are many good features in the Bristol One City COVID-19 communications strategy, three should be highlighted:

- First, while the City Council is hosting this website, the information provided is both holistic and user friendly. There are direct links to services provided by all manner of organizations – charities, the NHS, the police, central government, and so on.
- Second, much of the information is place-based and specific to Bristol. For example, there is information for NHS staff and care workers about how to park for free in City Council car parks and in RPZs.

- Third, the information is rapidly updated, to take account of changing circumstances, and the communications team makes extensive use of social media.

Mayor Rees has been issuing a coronavirus information and advice newsletter every week and, on top of that, he delivers a regular video update. Although short, these videos communicate key messages very clearly. It was obvious that the Mayor was broadcasting his advice from his home, and this conveyed an immediacy that many people, also constrained by lockdown, could relate to.

It is important to refer here to Can-Do Bristol, a city-wide platform for volunteering and social action. Launched by the Mayor in 2017, long before the COVID-19 outbreak emerged, the platform has been incredibly effective in organizing voluntary efforts since the pandemic struck the city.[39]

Turning to Bristol's strategic efforts relating to post COVID-19 recovery, it is difficult to overstate the importance of the six cross-sector boards set up to deliver the One City Plan. They provide the collaborative foundations for the creation of imaginative proposals and solutions. The six boards relate to: Connectivity; Economy; Environment; Health and Wellbeing; Homes and Communities; and Learning and Skills.

Thus, for example, the One City Economy Board, which started work in September 2019, is co-chaired by a Deputy Mayor and the Director of Business West (the local business association). The Board, which brings together representatives from all the realms of civic leadership shown in Figure 4.2, is actively delivering initiatives and projects designed to rebuild the Bristol economy in a more inclusive and more sustainable way.[40] After the pandemic hit the country, the Economy Board started meeting once a week and it launched *A One City economic renewal strategy* at the City Gathering on 26 June 2020.[41]

Meanwhile, the One City Environmental Sustainability Board, which first met in July 2019, has prepared a One City Climate Strategy, designed to develop a carbon–neutral Bristol by 2030.[42]

Extinction Rebellion, the increasingly influential, global environmental movement, has endorsed this ambitious strategy.[43] In May 2020, Bristol City Council, in line with steps taken in many other progressive cities around the world, announced plans to free the historic centre of Bristol from motor traffic.[44]

Conclusions

Before identifying key lessons emerging from the Bristol One City Approach to city governance, it is important to refer to the damaging impact of central government policies on all local authorities in the UK. As noted in Chapter Two, the Conservative government has sustained a decade-long attack on local democracy and local public services.[45] In the case of Bristol, the cut in central government financial support to the City Council was from £201 million a year in 2010–11 to £45 million a year in 2019–20 – that's a 78 per cent cut. Central government's misguided commitment to so-called 'austerity' meant that the City Council, alongside local authorities across the country, was forced to cut public spending and local services dramatically.

Despite the constraints, Bristol has developed an innovative approach to city governance and this has received international recognition. Each year, the European Union invites cities to put themselves forward for the award of European Capital of Innovation (iCapital). In September 2019, the Bristol One City Approach ensured that Bristol was recognized as one of the six most innovative cities in Europe.[46] As well as delivering a 100,000 euro cash prize to the city, this award suggested that Bristol's innovative approach to collaborative governance was, indeed, breaking new ground.

In Chapter One, I summarized three key lessons from previous disasters around the world, including insights provided by Lucy Jones from her study of earthquakes, and I revisit them here.[47] First, having good local governance arrangements in place before, during and after a disaster saves lives and underpins societal recovery. The civic leaders involved in developing and delivering the Bristol One City Approach will be the first to say that it can be improved. Indeed, this urge to innovate is central to the strategy that leaders have developed. Nevertheless, the evidence presented in this chapter suggests that Bristol's good governance arrangements are serving the city well.

Second, competent and committed place-based leaders can make a huge difference to governmental performance. Empathetic civic leaders can make an emotional connection with other actors – they know their city and are well placed to spur on collective action. The hundreds of civic leaders who participate in Bristol City Gatherings provide formidable leadership capacity. These leaders come from all five realms of civic leadership shown in Figure 4.2, and they are only the tip of the iceberg.

Third, the disaster studies literature suggests that cities and localities that look ahead, and develop a far-sighted vision for their area, are far better placed to respond to a crisis. They don't have to suddenly agree a vision and develop a collaborative strategy – they already have one. The Bristol One City Plan took over two years to co-create and, because it has substantial stakeholder buy-in, it provides an excellent platform for post COVID-19 recovery. More than that, because institutional arrangements were carefully built to deliver the plan – via City Gatherings and the creation of thematic boards – good relationships across the realms of civic leadership were already in place before the COVID-19 emergency struck. It is these relationships that are making a major contribution to the resilience of Bristol today.

Notes

[1] Hambleton R. (2015) *Leading the Inclusive City: Place-based innovation for a bounded planet*, Bristol: Policy Press.

[2] The COVID-19 pandemic has, in practice, altered local government electoral cycles in the UK. All local elections scheduled for May 2020 were cancelled. In the case of Bristol, this means that the mayor and all

the councillors elected to serve for four years in May 2016 have been asked to continue to serve until May 2021.

[3] *The Sunday Times Best Places to Live Guide*, 19 March 2017.

[4] Dresser M. and Ollerenshaw P. (eds) (1996) *The Making of Modern Bristol*, Bristol: Redcliffe Press; Dresser M. (2016) *Slavery Obscured: The social history of the slave trade in an English provincial port*, London: Bloomsbury Academic.

[5] Morgan K. (1996) 'The economic development of Bristol, 1700–1850', pp 48–75 in M. Dresser and P. Ollerenshaw (eds) *The Making of Modern Bristol*, Bristol: Redcliffe Press, p 57.

[6] Bristol City Council (2019) *Deprivation in Bristol 2019*. October, Bristol: Bristol City Council. https://www.bristol.gov.uk/documents /20182/32951/Deprivation+in+Bristol+2019.pdf/ff3e5492-9849-6300-b227-1bdff2779f80

[7] Bristol City Council (2019) *JSNA Health and Wellbeing Profile 2019/20*. July, Bristol: Bristol City Council. https://www.bristol.gov.uk/documents/20182/3849453/JSNA+2019+-+Life+expectancy+%28Updated+Jul+19%29.pdf/8c56e9e7-4099-6812-4664-a17ebad2bf61

[8] 'Chief Constable Andy Marsh on yesterday's Black Lives Matter demonstration in Bristol', Avon and Somerset Police, 8 June 2020.

[9] 'Statue of Edward Colston was "offensive" to me, says Mayor of Bristol', *The Telegraph*, *YouTube interview*, 8 June 2020. https://www.youtube.com/watch?v=WkmMoCIRuKU

[10] Golding N. (2020) 'Marvin Rees: It's the challenge of immobility we're taking on', *Local Government Chronicle*, 6 July.

[11] In 2012, Dr David Sweeting, University of Bristol, and I launched a longitudinal action/research project designed to assess the impact of introducing a mayoral form of governance into a city. The Bristol Civic Leadership Project provides details of our various policy reports: http://bristolcivicleadership.net. See also: Hambleton R. and Sweeting D. (2014) 'Innovation in urban political leadership. Reflections on the introduction of a directly-elected mayor in Bristol, UK', *Public Money and Management*, 34(5): 315–322; Sweeting D. and Hambleton R. (2020) 'The dynamics of depoliticisation in urban governance: Introducing a directly elected mayor', *Urban Studies*, 57(5): 1068–1086; and Sweeting D. (ed) (2017) *Directly Elected Mayors in Urban Governance*, Bristol: Policy Press.

[12] Sweeting D. (2017) 'Introduction: directly elected mayors in urban governance' in D. Sweeting (ed) *Directly Elected Mayors in Urban Governance*, Bristol: Policy Press, pp 4–5.

[13] Hambleton R. and Sweeting D. (2015) *The Impacts of Mayoral Governance in Bristol*. September. Report of the Bristol Civic Leadership Project. Bristol: University of Bristol. More: https://bristolcivicleadership.files.wordpress.com/2013/03/impacts-of-mayoral-governance-in-bristol-web-version.pdf

14 *The Mayor's Race* is a documentary film made by Loraine Blumenthal and Rob Mitchell, released in 2018. https://themayorsracefilm.com

15 See, for example: Royko M. (1988) *Boss: Richard J. Daley*, New York: Penguin; and Cohen A. and Taylor E. (2000) *American Pharaoh: Mayor Richard J. Daley: His battle for Chicago and the nation*, Boston MA: Little, Brown and Company.

16 This is not a new insight. Ross Ashby, an influential figure in cybernetics, formulated his Law of Requisite Variety in the early 1950s. See: Ashby W.R. (1956) *An Introduction to Cybernetics*, London: Chapman and Hall.

17 The super-centralization of power within Whitehall is extreme. See: Hambleton R. (2017) 'The super-centralisation of the English state – Why we need to move beyond the devolution deception', *Local Economy*, 32(1): 3–13.

18 The first Director of the Bristol City Office was David Relph, who, on a part-time basis, built local networks of support. In early 2019, Mayor Rees, notwithstanding the budget reductions being imposed by central government, created a City Office team comprising two part-time co-directors – Andrea Dell and Ed Rowberry – supported by two staff, David Ader and Annabel Smith. Additional support to the City Office was provided by seconded staff – notably Alan Macleod and David Barclay.

19 Morris S. (2017) 'Bristol launches "spectrum of activity" to tackle homelessness', *The Guardian*, 25 January.

20 For more details of the Feeding Bristol Healthy Holiday Programme, visit: https://www.feedingbristol.org/healthy-holidays

21 For more details on Period Friendly Bristol, visit: https://www.periodfriendlybristol.org

22 The Bristol One City Plan was launched in January 2019 and rolled forward in January 2020. For more details, visit: https://www.bristolonecity.com

23 The 2030 Agenda for Sustainable Development, adopted by the UN Member States in 2015, provides a shared blueprint for peace and prosperity for people and the planet: https://sustainabledevelopment.un.org/?menu=1300

24 Personal notes by the author, Bristol City Gathering, 10 January 2020.

25 For more details on the City Funds Board, visit: www.bristolcityfunds.co.uk

26 For more details on Bristol City Office leadership programmes, visit: https://www.bristol.gov.uk/mayor/city- office-leadership-programmes

27 Interview by the author, 9 January 2020, Bristol City Hall.

28 The Stepping Up programme has been shortlisted for a *Local Government Chronicle* national award for promoting diversity and inclusion. See: https://www.bristol.gov.uk/mayor/stepping-up-programme

[29] Boyer E.L. (1990) *Scholarship Reconsidered: Priorities of the professoriate*, Princeton, NJ: Carnegie Foundation for the Advancement of Teaching.

[30] I explore the theme of university engagement in the city in more detail in: Hambleton R. (2015) *Leading the Inclusive City. Place-based innovation for a bounded planet*, Bristol: Policy Press, pp 290–297.

[31] Hambleton R. (2018) 'British universities – the sleeping giants of place-based leadership?', *People, Place and Policy*, 12(1): 1–7.

[32] The author chaired this team, which came to be known as the Bristol Forum Planning Team.

[33] Hambleton R. (2019) 'How can the US experience advance the civic university', *Wonkhe*, 14 March. https://wonkhe.com/search/Robin+Hambleton

[34] For more on the Atlanta Studies Network, see: https://www.atlantastudies.org/network/

[35] The Bristol Forum was co-organized by the City Office, the University of Bristol and the University of the West of England, Bristol. http://bristolforum.org.uk

[36] Civic University Commission (2019) *Truly Civic: Strengthening the connection between universities and their places*, London: Civic University Commission.

[37] Launched in March 2020 the Civic University Network is designed to strengthen university civic engagement. See: https://www.shu.ac.uk/about-us/civic-university-network

[38] For more on the Bristol One City Approach, visit: https://www.bristolonecity.com

[39] For more on Can-Do Bristol, visit: https://candobristol.co.uk

[40] For more on the work of the Bristol One City Economy Board, see: https://www.bristolonecity.com/economy/the-economy-board/

[41] For more on the Bristol economic renewal strategy, visit: https://www.bristolonecity.com/wp-content/uploads/2020/06/One-City-Economic-Recovery-Statement-of-Intent.pdf

[42] For more on the work of the Bristol One City Environmental Sustainability Board, see: https://www.bristolonecity.com/environment/the-environment-board/

[43] Extinction Rebellion, as an organization, does not endorse any particular political parties, but they have backed the Bristol One City Climate Strategy. More: https://xrbristol.org.uk/2020/03/11/our-support-of-the-one-city-climate-strategy-is-beyond-party-politics/

[44] Morris S. (2020) 'A giant leap for pedestrians as Bristol plans for car-free centre', *The Guardian*, 22 May.

[45] Latham P. (2017) *Who Stole the Town Hall? The end of local government as we know it*, Bristol: Policy Press.

46 For more on European iCapital 2019, see: https://ec.europa.eu/info/research-and-innovation/funding/funding-opportunities/prizes/icapital/icapital-2019_en

47 Jones L. (2018) *The Big Ones: How natural disasters have shaped humanity*, London: Icon Books Ltd.

SIX

Enhancing
the International Conversation

Introduction

The COVID-19 pandemic presents a global challenge and it follows that an effective societal response must involve international collaboration.

In Chapter Three, I expressed concern about the way national governments are not, as yet, working that well together. Indeed, there has been a troubling growth in nationalism in recent years, and this makes the vital work of very important international bodies, such as the UN and the WHO, all the more difficult. In this chapter, we will explore the growth of international networking by sub-national units of government. At this level of governance, the outlook for fruitful international exchange and collaboration is altogether brighter.

Benjamin Barber advanced the view that city mayors, singly or jointly, are more capable of responding to transnational challenges than nation states, mainly because they are not mired in ideological infighting and sovereign rivalries.[1] Indeed, he argued that the nation state is failing us on a global scale, not least because it is utterly unsuited to interdependence. The way that politicians leading nation states are finding it so difficult to work together in responding to the COVID-19 pandemic lends support to Barber's analysis. It could well be that, as Barber argues, in today's globalizing world the city has become democracy's best hope.

The focus of this chapter is, then, on international dialogue *below* the level of the nation state. There has, in fact, been a spectacular rise in international city-to-city learning and exchange, and this multifaceted process is leading to widespread innovation in collaborative governance, citizen empowerment and community leadership.[2] The presentation unfolds in three steps.

First, the reasons why cities and localities engage in international exchange are set out, and the potential of cross-border lesson drawing for improving public policy and societal innovation is highlighted. Reference is made to some of the many international local government and city networks that now play an increasingly important role in assisting place-to-place dialogue and learning.

The second section provides the heart of this chapter. It presents short 'innovation cameos' of five cities drawn from five different countries, to illustrate the way in which place-based leaders in specific localities are, right now, developing imaginative responses to the complex challenges facing us. These cities are chosen because, in line with the argument presented in Chapter Three, they provide insights on how to improve the quality of city governance. An innovation cameo, in this context, is a very short account of the way in which a particular city or locality is governed, and how it is breaking new ground in responding to current societal challenges. The evidence suggests that effective responses to the COVID-19 pandemic need to address – at the same time – pre-existing challenges relating to, for example, the climate change emergency, corrosive social inequality and systemic racism.

Third, a concluding section highlights the importance of international place-to-place learning and exchange. It suggests that universities across the world could become much more active in collaborating with actors in the place where they are located and, as part of this, they could be more vigorous in bringing their research skills to bear on efforts to improve the quality of international lesson drawing.

Why should place-based leaders look abroad?

There are three main reasons why place-based leaders benefit from investing time and effort in understanding what civic leaders in other countries are doing:

- international lesson drawing
- international relationship building
- enhancing place-based power[3]

International lesson drawing

First, a key reason for much modern city-to-city international networking is lesson drawing for public policy development and policy implementation. This involves examining experiences in cities and regions in one or more other countries, in order to discover relevant new insights for policy and practice in the home city.[4] International city-to-city lesson drawing can deliver a number of potential benefits for policy makers:

- First, experience abroad can act as an invaluable source of practical and useful ideas.
- Second, while cities may be faced with common problems, it is clear that these problems do not produce identical policy responses. It is the differences in responses that different cities make to shared problems that can provide stimulating, even inspiring, insights for civic leaders.
- Third, in a world in which unprecedented numbers of people are now migrating across national boundaries, cross-national exchange can lift the level of local intercultural knowledge, awareness and understanding.

I offer a word of caution to civic leaders who decide to embark on international lesson drawing efforts. As they search for new insights from the experiences of localities in other countries, it is essential that they reject the idea of 'best practice' in local governance. There is no such thing. Elsewhere, I have set out five arguments why, when it comes to policy development and urban innovation, the idea of 'best practice' should be replaced by the idea of 'relevant practice'.[5] Places vary, political cultures vary and to suggest that there is a 'best' solution is a denial of the richness and diversity of modern life. Worse than that, the notion of 'best practice' pushes intellectual effort in the wrong direction. It creates the false impression that the 'best' answer is out there – somebody else has already discovered it for us. On the contrary, innovative civic leaders should examine foreign experience in order to prompt fresh thinking which can, in turn, help local actors to co-create entirely new solutions. My suggestion is that place-based leaders should be encouraged to scan experience elsewhere, in order to discover insights that are *relevant* to the challenges they face in their own locality.

International competitions designed to recognize good examples of city leadership, urban planning and social innovation can generate practical suggestions. For example, in Europe cities compete for the award of European Green Capital and European Capital of Innovation.[6] On a global scale, international city competitions include the Lee Kuan Yew World City Prize and the Guangzhou International Award for Urban Innovation.[7]

International relationship building

If international lesson drawing is carried out well, it can lead to international relationship building. Such relationships can be binary pairings, as in sister-city or town-twinning arrangements, or clusters of cities focusing on a particular topic or theme. For example, the C40 cities network was set up in 2005 to tackle the climate change emergency, and the Cities

Alliance, founded in 1999, is a global partnership focused on urban poverty reduction.[8] The growth of international city-to-city networks designed to help cities build relationships has been remarkable. In 1985, there were roughly 60 international city networks; now there are over 300.[9]

A good example of a European network of cities is provided by EUROCITIES. Founded in 1986, EUROCITIES, initially a grouping of six cities, is now an influential network of around 140 European cities, with over 45 partner cities outside Europe. The network has developed a good platform for city-to-city sharing of ideas on how to respond to the COVID-19 pandemic.[10] Other place-based international networks offer similar advice and assistance – see, for example, United Cities and Local Governments, the International Council for Local Environmental Initiatives and the UN World Urban Forum.[11]

Enhancing place-based power

In Chapter One, I suggested that place-less power has grown significantly in the last thirty years or so. This expansion in the power of place-less decision makers (meaning individuals and organizations who are unconcerned about the impact of their decisions on communities living in particular places) has diminished the power of elected local leaders in most, if not all countries. Added to the attack on local power by multinational companies, elected local authorities in some countries also find themselves battered by their central governments. The growing centralization of legal and fiscal power within some nation states has weakened the power of place. For example, in England, as discussed in Chapter Two, the ruthless cutting of central government financial support to elected local authorities since 2010, coupled with a super-centralization of detailed decision making in Whitehall, has brought about a shocking decline in the power of place in the country.[12]

Faced with external threats of this kind, many city leaders are fighting back, by working with colleagues in other countries to expand the power of all places. Thus, some of the international networks linking cities together represent deliberate efforts to strengthen the power of cities and city regions in the dynamics of global governance. This growth of city diplomacy is becoming increasingly visible.[13] Moreover, new international city groupings with the explicit aim of expanding city power – for example, the Global Parliament of Mayors; and Mayors Migration Council – have emerged in recent years.[14]

International examples of inspirational civic leadership

Can we unearth examples of inspirational place-based leadership that provide promising practical ideas on how to co-construct a progressive post COVID-19 world? The fact is that there are thousands of elected local authorities across the world that are working with their communities to respond, in an imaginative way, to the complex challenges they now face. Bold innovations are taking place in many localities, and the international associations, mentioned earlier, play an important role in facilitating international exchange.

In this section, in the limited space available, I draw attention to five examples of inspirational place-based leadership. The aim here is to identify cities of varying size that are delivering on the progressive values that I outlined in Chapter Three. All the cities presented here are, then, trying to create inclusive cities. Alongside a commitment to creating fairer cities, they all stress caring for the natural environment on which we all depend. Some of the cities are fairly small – for example, Dunedin, New Zealand, has a population of 132,000 – while others are larger. Some have directly elected mayors, some don't. Some have substantial local autonomy to decide on priorities and investments – for example, Freiburg, Germany – while others have less place-based power. What unites them is that they are all progressive and innovative.

My hope is that these 'innovation cameos' can stimulate fresh thinking. They are short and follow a standard format: Opening; Overview; Responding to COVID-19; and Lesson drawing. Sources are provided at the end of each cameo for those who wish to follow up. The five cities are:

- Innovation Cameo 1: Copenhagen, Denmark
- Innovation Cameo 2: Dunedin, New Zealand
- Innovation Cameo 3: Freiburg, Germany
- Innovation Cameo 4: Mexico City, Mexico
- Innovation Cameo 5: Portland, Oregon, US

INNOVATION CAMEO 1

City of cyclists – Copenhagen, Denmark

Opening

Copenhagen is widely recognized as one of the most liveable cities in the world. For example, in January 2020, Health Europa designated Copenhagen as the healthiest capital city in Europe.[1] In Copenhagen, there are now more bicycles than cars and the city aims to become the world's first carbon-neutral capital by 2025. We will focus here on the way community organizations have put pressure on civic leaders in Copenhagen to expand the public realm and, in particular, encouraged cycling. Promoting cycling is a particularly effective way of responding to the COVID-19 emergency. Cyclists incur less risk of infection and, of course, cycling is a good strategy for reducing obesity levels in the population – a core risk factor in relation to COVID-19.

Overview

Denmark leads the world on climate change action, having reduced its CO_2 emissions by more than half, since peaking in 1996. The country is now ranked number one in the world on the independent global Environmental Performance Index.[2] Copenhagen won the award of European Green Capital in 2014 and the city has, since the 1960s, established a solid reputation for designing and creating a people-friendly city.[3] Jan Gehl and Lars Gemzoe, two imaginative urban designers, contributed a great deal to the reshaping of the public realm in Copenhagen.[4]

The government of Copenhagen, a municipality with a population of 603,000 within a metropolitan area of 1.3 million, consists of a City Council, with 55 members elected for a term of four years, and seven standing committees.[5] The city's electoral system uses proportional representation. The most important committee is the Finance Committee. Chaired by the Lord Mayor, Frank Jensen, it comprises the six Deputy Mayors plus six members of the City Council. Importantly, all six standing committees have the power to take decisions within their portfolio. The City Council meets every fortnight.

This highly participatory model of city governance has delivered a biking revolution in Copenhagen.[6] Community activism has driven progressive change. A key feature in the governance of the city has been the use of ambitious place-based targets, coupled with rigorous monitoring of performance. In relation to cycling, for example, in 1996 the City Council introduced a system of bi-annual indicators (known as the Bicycling Account). This process has provided the traffic department with rich data, not just on bicycle use in the city, but also on Copenhageners' perceptions of cycling conditions.

Responding to the COVID-19 challenge

Like other cities across the world, Copenhagen has developed a user-friendly information service for citizens on the City Council website. This provides information on city operations and access to a range of hotlines for those needing assistance.

Lesson drawing

- Truly radical change can be achieved, if community-based organizations adopt a persistent approach in pressing for progressive innovation.
- A collective model of city leadership can work very well.
- Rigorous and ongoing research relating to public behaviour and actual performance can underpin policy development – for example, Bicycle Accounts and Green Accounts.
- An inclusive approach, emphasizing open communication and involving a range of ways of learning from different interest groups in the city, means that policies can be modified to respond to changing perceptions.
- It helps if central government is supportive of city-level efforts to advance progressive aims and objectives.

Notes

1   Health Europa (2020) 'Copenhagen crowned Europe's healthiest capital city', 21 January. https://www.healtheuropa.eu/copenhagen-crowned-europes-healthiest-city/96778/
2   The Environmental Performance Index ranks 180 countries in the world, using 32 performance indicators across 11 categories. https://epi.yale.edu
3   I discuss Copenhagen's achievements in more detail in: Hambleton R. (2015) *Leading the Inclusive City: Place-based innovation for a bounded planet*, Bristol: Policy Press, pp 246–250.
4   Gehl J. and Gemzoe L. (1996) *Public Spaces – Public Life: Copenhagen 1996*, Copenhagen: The Danish Architectural Press.
5   Municipality of Copenhagen (2018) *The City of Copenhagen Government 2018–2021.* https://international.kk.dk/artikel/city-copenhagen-government
6   Nielson T.A.S., Skov-Petersen H. and Carstensen T.A. (2013) 'Urban planning practices for bikeable cities – the case of Copenhagen', *Urban Research and Practice*, 6(1): 110–115.

INNOVATION CAMEO 2

Going green in Dunedin, New Zealand

Opening

Ōtepoti Dunedin is a diverse and progressive city, located in the South Island of New Zealand. Indigenous Māori first settled there nearly 1,000 years ago, while the influence of Scottish settlers in the mid-19th century can still be seen in the city today – particularly in the educational and cultural institutions for which Dunedin is renowned. In 2019, the citizens elected the first Green Party mayor in Australasia. Aaron Hawkins was 35 years old when he took office and, by exercising outgoing collaborative leadership, he is orchestrating a number of initiatives designed to respond in an imaginative way to the COVID-19 emergency.

Overview

The directly elected mayor model of governance was introduced into New Zealand by the Municipal Corporations Act 1876. This model provides for the direct election of the leader of the city by the citizens, as well as the election of city councillors to serve on the city council. In Dunedin, population 132,000, the mayor and the 14 councillors are elected for a three-year term.[1] Hawkins, who has been a member of the

Green Party since 2010 and a city councillor since 2013, summarized his aims in an interview given to Bruce Munro shortly after he was elected: "Dunedin needs to become a zero carbon city that looks after its people".[2]

Hawkins is a colourful character, who is deeply committed to tackling the climate change emergency. As a city councillor and now mayor, his practice of regularly hitch hiking to and from the City Council from his home in Port Chalmers, eight miles to the north Dunedin, is eco-friendly and provides opportunities for him to talk to local people on the 20-minute ride. Since being elected, he has turned down having a mayoral car. In his interview with Munro, he described his approach to city leadership: "I think my leadership style is collaborative. Having different and divergent views around the council table is healthy. It is important those views are heard in a way that is collegial and constructive."

Responding to the COVID-19 challenge

The New Zealand Local Government Act 2002 ensures that all local authorities engage their communities in both long-term and annual planning. This ongoing process ensures that localities across the country have a pretty clear sense of direction. Hawkins has indicated that he wants to build on the plans already in place, but also recognizes that policies need to be adapted to address pressing COVID-19 challenges. In May 2020, Dunedin City Council approved a set of very innovative, albeit controversial, place-making measures, to encourage citizens to return to the city centre following the lifting of the lockdown. Traffic-calming measures included a radical reduction of the speed limit, to 10kmh, on the main street. Road space was freed up for pedestrians and hospitality businesses.[3] Hawkins and his council have also introduced a significant COVID-19 Recovery Fund, to support the community's social and economic wellbeing in the wake of the pandemic.

Lesson drawing

- Local leaders play a significant role in shaping COVID-19 response and recovery strategies.
- The directly elected mayor model of local governance enhances the political legitimacy of the person elected to lead a city, expanding scope for innovative and progressive responses by mayors and their communities.

- National legislation mandating regular long-term and annual planning by elected local authorities, enriched by requirements for a high level of civic participation, provides a mechanism for strengthening anticipatory governance to address future challenges.
- Taking steps to respond to COVID-19 challenges can, and should, be aligned with efforts to tackle the present global climate emergency.

Notes

1 For more on Dunedin City Council, visit: https://www.dunedin.govt.nz
2 Munro B. (2019) 'The top job', *Otago Daily Times*, 21 October. https://www.odt.co.nz/lifestyle/magazine/top-job
3 McNeilly H. (2020) 'Covid-19 prompts Dunedin council to consider reducing CBD speed to just 10kmh', *Stuff*, 20–26 May. https://www.stuff.co.nz/national/politics/local-government/121488595/covid19-prompts-dunedin-council-to-consider-reducing-cbd-speed-to-just-10kmh?rm=a

INNOVATION CAMEO 3

Good planning in Freiburg, Germany

Opening

Freiburg, Germany's southernmost city, has established itself as a world leader in relation to sustainable development. The city, which has a population of 230,000, has been successful in promoting a civic culture that combines a very strong commitment to green values and respect for nature, with a buoyant economy built around, among other things, renewable energy. The UK-based Academy of Urbanism was so impressed with the achievements of the city that it published *The Freiburg Charter for Sustainable Urbanism* to promote imaginative city planning and sound urban design.[1]

Overview

The origins of the community activism that underpins current innovations in Freiburg can be traced back to the late 1970s. A successful local and regional campaign against a proposal to locate a nuclear power station in nearby Wyhl provided the original impetus. A colourful coalition of anti-nuclear activists was born and, from small beginnings, this peaceful, green movement became increasingly successful.

Freiburg has a directly elected mayor, who serves for a fixed term of eight years, and a city council (*Gemeinderat*) with 48 members elected on an 'at large' basis for a term of five years. Local authorities in Germany are relatively strong – they have a constitutional right to local self-government and they have the legal power to levy their own taxes to finance activities, as they think fit.

Over a long period, politicians, planners, the local university, businesses, community groups and civil society in general have worked well together in Freiburg. The city has an integrated land use/transport strategy.[2] All major trip generators have to be located close to a tram stop, and the publicly owned tram system is superb. There are no out-of-town retail developments or business parks. From having no bike paths in 1970, the city now has over 300 miles of bike lanes. There is a high level of citizen participation, and neighbourhoods are designed in a child-friendly way. The results are impressive. Green initiatives are everywhere and car ownership, already well below the German average, is falling.[3]

In 2018, Martin Horn, a young Social Democratic Party politician, was elected Mayor of Freiburg and, among other things, he has pushed forward policies designed to create more affordable housing in the city.

Responding to the COVID-19 challenge

Because Freiburg has a relatively good system of urban governance, it was well placed to respond to the COVID-19 outbreak. Many excellent community-based initiatives are now under way. An imaginative effort designed to use digital communication technologies to strengthen community resilience and civic engagement stands out. The *Freiburg hält zusammen* (*Freiburg holds together*) digital network, launched in April 2020, bundles together numerous citizen-oriented information services and activities.[4] The data shared, relating to, for example, neighbourhood help or local work, is driven by social purpose, not commercial interest. The university has played a key role in working with partners to develop this new system.

Lesson drawing

- German local authorities have substantial legal and fiscal autonomy to respond flexibly to new challenges. This creates local political space for bold public innovation.

- Huge increases in land value accrue from development planning decisions. These gains are used for essential infrastructure, to the benefit of citizens and local businesses.
- Civic leaders from inside and outside the state have developed an imaginative vision of what they want their city to be like in the future and they work in a collaborative way to achieve this common goal.

Notes

1 Academy of Urbanism and Stadt Freiburg (2012) *The Freiburg Charter for Sustainable Urbanism* (2nd edn), London: Academy of Urbanism.
2 Daseking W. (2014) 'Freiburg: Principles of sustainable development', *Journal of Urban Regeneration and Renewal*, 8(2): 145–151.
3 For more on Freiburg's achievements, see: Hall P. (2013) *Good Cities, Better Lives: How Europe discovered the lost art of urbanism*, Abingdon: Routledge, pp 248–273; and Hambleton R. (2015) *Leading the Inclusive City: Place-based innovation for a bounded planet.* Bristol: Policy Press, pp 228–232.
4 For more on the 'Freiburg holds together' innovation, see https://www.freiburg.de/pb/1542745.html

INNOVATION CAMEO 4

Doing errands in Mexico City, Mexico

Arturo Flores, Universidad Anáhuac, Mexico City

Opening

Mexico City, with a population of 8.9 million within a metropolitan area of over 20 million, is a massive, complex city with a longstanding reputation for social innovation. Many of these transformations have been prompted by natural disasters as well as economic or political calamities. The evidence suggests that citizens become particularly active when they are faced with major setbacks and/or intolerable injustices.

Overview

The origins of the social changes that are now taking place in Mexico City can be traced back to the 1968 student movement. Tragically, on 2 October 1968, a public demonstration against various injustices ended with the killing of a large number of students in the *Plaza de las Tres Culturas*. In the years that followed, social movements continued to raise concerns about the governance of the city. In September

1985, a terrible earthquake spurred an upsurge in public protest and expressions of citizen anger, and the event became a landmark in the development of participatory politics in Mexico City.

Political campaigning for increased local democracy continued and, in 1997, the citizens of Mexico City won the right to be able to elect the mayor of the city, as well as members of the Legislative Assembly. Ever since then, Mexico City has been ruled by left-leaning political parties and, over time, the city has established a reputation for being progressive. For example, in 2009, Mexico City became the first Latin American jurisdiction to legalize same-sex marriage. In 2010, an ambitious participatory budgeting system was introduced, providing for the active participation of over 1,800 communities in decision making relating to how to spend 3 per cent of the budget's capital.[1]

Responding to the COVID-19 challenge

An example of community response to the COVID-19 emergency is provided by a group of young people who have created the @ HagoMandadosMX ('I do errands MX') initiative. The aim is to support citizens who are required to stay at home following the lockdown introduced by the health authority. They use their bicycles and motorcycles to provide services to residents of four local authorities in Mexico City. Their 'office' is a bench in Plaza Luis Cabrera, in Roma. These young people wait to be contacted by message or Twitter to run errands. They made an alliance with five restaurants to do food deliveries. They also run errands to pharmacies; pay electricity, gas and water bills; transport pet food; deliver toys; and do supermarket shopping.[2]

Lesson drawing

- The people of Mexico City are remarkably resilient, and citizens demonstrate a great capacity to promote social innovations whenever a crisis takes place.
- Local leadership often stems from actors who are outside the state, and seems to emerge to fill gaps in local authority services.
- The introduction of participatory budgeting in 2010, while not perfect, did stimulate citizens to engage in decision-making processes at the local level.

Notes

1   Flores A. (2016) 'Mexico City and its participatory budget: A truly empowering process of citizen participation?' in Y. Beebeejaun (ed) *The Participatory City*, Berlin: Jovis Verlag GmbH, pp 38–45.
2   Cited from Twitter account @HagoMandadosMX (3 April 2020); see also www.reforma.com.

INNOVATION CAMEO 5

Progressive politics in Portland, Oregon, US

Opening

Portland, Oregon, US, has acquired an international reputation for progressive policy making. A city of 610,000 in a metropolitan area of 2.4 million, Portland has a long-established commitment to sustainable urban development.[1] The city was the first in the US to adopt a firm position on climate change – it set ambitious targets for the reduction of greenhouse gas emissions in 1993. Ted Wheeler, Mayor of Portland, has built on the work of his predecessors and has been one of the many American city leaders opposing President Donald Trump's divisive policies. However, the summer of 2020 confronted the city with four major challenges at once: the COVID-19 health emergency; a very sharp economic downturn arising from the pandemic; the climate emergency; and an upsurge in community anger about continuing systemic racism following the death of George Floyd while being arrested by police officers in Minneapolis on 25 May 2020.

Overview

Portland has an unusual system of governance. It is the only large US city to retain a commission form of government. The city has six directly elected officials: the mayor, four commissioners and the auditor.[2] The mayor is the directly elected leader of the city, but this is not a strong mayor model. The mayor has to share power and civic leadership responsibilities with other directly elected officials. Community activism in the neighbourhoods of Portland is well developed, and citizen involvement in decision making is an important part of the civic culture.

As well as tackling climate change, the city has also tried to address issues relating to social justice. For example, in 2011 a city-level Office of Equity and Human Rights was created, to elevate considerations relating to fairness in the city to a central position within political debates. Notwithstanding these efforts, on 28 May 2020, Portland was one of the first US cities to witness major civil disturbances following the death of George Floyd. For weeks after this initial protest, there were daily peaceful demonstrations – as well as destruction of property and looting by a minority of citizens.

The City Council has taken bold steps to respond to the Black Lives Matter protests. On 8 June 2020, Jami Resch, the chief of police, stepped down and was replaced by Chuck Lovell. On 17 June, influenced by the remarkable leadership shown by Commissioner Jo Ann Hardesty, the city council agreed to reduce the Portland Police Bureau's budget by $27 million in total, and to redirect expenditures to develop a new approach to public safety in the city.[3]

Responding to the COVID-19 challenge

Portland City Council acted quickly to provide information and support to local people about COVID-19 and, on 20 May 2020, approved a COVID-19 Response Values Framework, setting out the desire to prioritize the hardest-hit community members.

Lesson drawing

- Civic leaders in Portland have demonstrated their willingness to listen to public protests and respond in an empathetic way. The mayor and the city council dramatically changed their position on, for example, budget priorities in a matter of a few weeks.
- By organizing a sustained and largely peaceful campaign, civic activists and campaigners have helped the city to consider how to become more effective in caring for everyone in the city.
- A commission form of government enables different voices to be heard at the very top level, and this diversity of opinion helped the city to take radical steps forward.

Notes

1 Ozawa C.P. (2004) *The Portland Edge: Challenges and successes in growing communities*, Washington DC: Island Press.
2 More on Portland City Government: https://www.portlandoregon.gov/25783
3 On 17 June 2020, Commissioner Hardesty gave a remarkable speech, in which she pleaded with community activists to recognize the complexity of the issues facing the city. https://www.youtube.com/watch?time_continue=7320&v=4EleA-8LWdE&feature=emb_logo

Conclusions

The COVID-19 pandemic, a global menace, requires an international response. When commenting on the need for international action in relation to the current climate emergency, Caroline Lucas MP, the only Green Party Member of Parliament in the UK, expressed views that are equally important in relation to the COVID-19 pandemic:

> 'The crises we face will not be solved by one country alone, but by leaders of all nations speaking out together for urgent and radical change. It's time for politicians to stop arguing among themselves, stop blaming their opponents and unite behind the need for transformative change.'[15]

It is disappointing to record that the leaders of nation states, even in the face of the COVID-19 calamity, have, as yet, failed to construct a coherent international response to the pandemic, let alone to climate change, and still less the unacceptable levels of inequality that now disfigure life in even the most wealthy countries in the world.

Given this weakness in effective international collaborative leadership, it looks as if the leaders of cities and communities will need to take on the challenge of world leadership. It is encouraging to record that there has been a marked rise in the volume and intensity of international city-to-city dialogue and exchange in the last twenty years or so. There are, right now, thousands of cities and communities pushing ahead with important efforts to help their localities respond to the COVID-19 pandemic and to develop forward strategies. As noted in Chapter One, many city mayors and local leaders around the world are acutely aware of the international dimension of their work, and are actively implementing a variety of 'Think globally, act locally' strategies. In some cases, they are not just thinking globally, they are acting globally as well as locally.

Marvin Rees, Mayor of Bristol, is active on the international stage in a variety of roles, particularly within the Global Parliament of Mayors and the Mayors Migration Council. In 2019, I asked him 'Why should city leaders spend time and effort on international work?' and he outlined two main reasons:

'One is because we have international populations. If I'm going to represent the interests of people in Bristol I can't stop at the city's boundaries, because the people of Bristol are international ... they're Somali, Jamaican, Pakistani, Bangladeshi, Chinese and more, and they're interested in what's happening for their family and people around the world ... The next is that what goes on outside Bristol shapes Bristol, be it financial flows, people movements, climate change, what's going on in terms of the economy and developments in national and international policy ... so we have to be able to shape those things for the good of the city ...'[16]

In closing this chapter, I would like to refer, albeit very briefly, to the role of universities and scholars, in enhancing international understanding of the challenges now facing cities and communities across the world. During the last twenty years or so, there has been a welcome rise in international academic analysis of urban and regional trends, challenges and issues, and new international networks of urban and environmental scholars have emerged. For example, the European Urban Research Association, founded in 1997, provides an international resource for sharing understanding.[17] More than that, there has been a growth in engaged scholarship, meaning scholarship that is focused on the co-creation of understanding and of ideas for action involving close collaboration between academics and non-campus actors.

Many universities now see themselves as civic universities – meaning that the university sees itself as an important place-based institution and devotes energy and resources to improving the quality of life in the area where it is located. This idea, long established in the US, is proving attractive to universities in other countries.[18]

These developments are all encouraging, and it is to be hoped that universities can become even more active in analyzing local challenges and co-creating solutions. When it comes to enhancing international city-to-city conversations, universities can contribute their research skills. This would help to improve the quality of international place-to-place learning and exchange in the future.

Notes

[1]   Barber B.R. (2013) *If Mayors Ruled the World: Dysfunctional nations, rising cities*, New Haven CT: Yale University Press.

[2]   Campbell T. (2012) *Beyond Smart Cities: How cities network, learn and innovate*, London: Earthscan; Van den Dool L. (ed) (2020) *Strategies for Urban Network Learning: International practices and theoretical reflections*, London: Palgrave Macmillan.

[3]   The different ways of engaging in international lesson drawing are explored in more detail in: Hambleton R. (2015) *Leading the Inclusive City: Place-based innovation for a bounded planet*, Bristol: Policy Press, pp 309–328.

[4]   Rose R. (2005) *Learning from Comparative Public Policy: A practical guide*, Abingdon: Routledge.

[5]   Hambleton R. (2020) 'From "best practice" to "relevant practice" in international city-to-city learning' in L. Van den Dool (ed) (2020) *Strategies for Urban Network Learning: International practices and theoretical reflections*, London: Palgrave Macmillan, pp 31–56.

[6]   European Green Capital: https://ec.europa.eu/environment/europeangreencapital/ and European Capital of Innovation: https://ec.europa.eu/info/research-and-innovation/funding/funding-opportunities/prizes/icapital_en

[7]   Lee Kuan Yew world City Prize: https://www.leekuanyewworldcityprize.com.sg and Guangzhou International Award for Urban Innovation: www.guangzhouaward.org

[8]   C40: https://www.c40knowledgehub.org/s/?language=en_US and Cities Alliance: Cities without slums: https://citiesalliance.org

9   Foster S.R. and Swiney C.F. (2019) *City Power and Powerlessness on the Global Stage*, Barcelona: CIDOB Barcelona Centre for International Affairs.

10 EUROCITIES: www.eurocities.eu

11 United Cities and Local Governments: https://www.uclg.org/; International Council for Local Environmental Initiatives: https://www.iclei.org; and World Urban Forum: https://wuf.unhabitat.org/

12 The super-centralization of power within England is extreme. See: Latham P. (2017) *Who Stole the Town Hall? The end of local government as we know it*, Bristol: Policy Press; and Hambleton R. (2017) 'The super-centralisation of the English state – Why we need to move beyond the devolution deception', *Local Economy*, 32(1): 3–13.

13 The Chicago Council on Global Affairs provides a noteworthy example. See: https://www.globalcitiesforum.org

14 Global Parliament of Mayors: https://globalparliamentofmayors.org and Mayors Migration Council: https://www.mayorsmigrationcouncil.org

15 Caroline Lucas MP is the only Green Party Member of Parliament in the UK. Lucas C. (2019) 'A political view' in Extinction Rebellion Handbook, *This Is Not A Drill*, London: Penguin, p 145.

16 Personal interview in Bristol City Hall, 17 July 2019.

17 The European Urban Research Association (EURA) has an academic journal, *Urban Research and Practice*, and a website that is being used to share ideas on the impact of the COVID-19 pandemic: https://eura.org

18 See, for example: Civic University Commission (2019) *Truly Civic: Strengthening the connection between universities and their places*, London: Civic University Commission.

SEVEN

Lesson Drawing for the Future

Introduction

The starting point for this final chapter is that we, human-kind, have played an influential role in causing the COVID-19 pandemic. Some appear to believe that we have just been hit by misfortune, that bad things happen and we can't do much about a strange virus that came out of nowhere. People who hold this view are misguided. In Chapter Two, I explained how the relentless exploitation of people and the planet, an uncaring and thoughtless approach that has dominated modern capitalism for much of the last forty years, has led directly to the appalling situation we now find ourselves in.

Mark Honigsbaum, in his forensic analysis of pandemics during the 20th century, shows how misguided exploitation of the planet has, repeatedly, disturbed the ecological equilibriums in which pathogens reside, and that these disruptions have then caused diseases.[1] Added to this, the massive expansion of factory farming has delivered not only widespread animal cruelty and abuse, but also a rocket boost to the virulence of zoonotic viruses, making them far more dangerous.[2] Pandemics, as well as the global climate catastrophe, arise from the misguided behaviour of human beings: we are the architects of our own suffering.

The good news is that, if human beings caused the pan-demic, we can, by modifying our behaviours and our public policies and practices, change things for the future. We can take steps to both reduce the chances of unforeseen calamities happening and, just as important, we can design governance arrangements that will strengthen our capacity to cope much more effectively with future disasters. We can, then, be the architects of a gentler, kinder world, one in which we all tread more lightly on the planet.

In this book, I have argued that the COVID-19 pandemic raises challenges for all societies that go far beyond public health and economics. I have suggested that the central issue that now confronts us is more profound than any particular public policy concern – it is the viability of democracy itself. On the one hand, if we refresh and revitalize our arrangements for democratic governance, then societies can take on the vested interests that continue to exploit people and the planet in an intolerable way. On the other hand, failure to reform our governance arrangements and, in particular, failure to take steps to control the malign behaviour of irresponsible people and organisations, will pave the way for continuing societal and environmental distress.

In this final chapter, I provide six pointers or suggestions that, when taken together, can prompt fresh thinking about future possibilities for an altogether better post COVID-19 world. The ideas set out here draw inspiration from the way in which communities, both nearby and in distant lands, have come together in a huge variety of ways to deal with the COVID-19 threat. We have all witnessed many remarkable acts of kindness and compassion in recent months, and the proliferation of examples of people caring for strangers has been uplifting. As argued by Rutger Bregman, it just might be that people are compassionate, not selfish, and that the instinct to cooperate rather than compete with each other has a deep evolutionary basis.[3]

There is no suggestion here that these proposals amount to a comprehensive strategy for reform. Moreover, my aim is not to spell out solutions – it is difficult enough to hint at a grammar that the reader can revise and develop in the light of her or his own experience.[4] However, I hope that these ideas about the importance of strengthening place-based power and enabling people in local communities to be far more influential in driving social change can be helpful.

Shifting the window of political possibilities

At various points in this book, I have suggested that the problems societies now face are extremely complex. It follows that simplistic slogans, while they may be attractive to populist politicians, are unlikely to provide a sound foundation for future public policy. The investigation of the COVID-19 pandemic presented in earlier chapters suggests that modern societies face, at least, four major interrelated challenges at the same time:

- the COVID-19 health emergency;
- a sharp economic downturn arising from the pandemic;
- the ongoing climate emergency;
- the rise of unacceptable inequality in modern societies, including the continuation of systemic racism.

To tackle these complex challenges successfully will require a substantial culture change within big business as well as wise political leadership and sound public management at international, national and local levels. Lasting solutions need societies to develop much more effective approaches to multi-level governance.

However, in the absence of sustained public pressure and community action, essential changes in governance will not come about. Vested interests will fight to suppress citizen voices advocating progressive change. It follows that would-be reformers should analyze current power structures and systems in an unflinching way. Stephen Lukes provides an excellent analysis of power in modern societies and, in particular, I want to highlight his suggestion that established power holders can be very effective in preventing radical ideas ever reaching the public arena in the first place.[5] This is why the window of political possibilities that I introduced in Chapter Three is so important. The key challenge facing our post COVID-19 world is to move this window towards a more caring perspective (see Figure 3.3).

The COVID-19 pandemic has reminded us that our well-being is not down to us as individuals – it is social. We are all interdependent, and our quality of life depends on us making intelligent decisions that support the common good. We can make each other ill or well. Figure 3.3 shows that the political window of possibilities can be moved, either towards exploitation of people and the planet or in the opposite direction. Here is a suggestion. As each specific policy proposal is put forward for consideration in every locality, city or nation state, a simple question can be asked: 'Does this proposal move us towards caring for others and the planet or not?' The key value here is caring. If the policy does not advance societal caring, decision makers can ask themselves: 'Why should we support this?'

It is encouraging to be able to record that vast numbers of people in thousands of cities and localities across the world are striving to build a caring society in the broadest sense. The international trade union movement deserves particular praise in this context. For example, in the UK the TUC has published useful suggestions on how to build a stronger, fairer economy.[6] The way in which communities and trade unions have responded to the COVID-19 emergency through community-based action is heart warming and encouraging. Unfortunately, a major obstacle lies in their path: place-less power.

Taking on place-less power

In the opening chapter, I introduced the notion of place-less power. Over the last thirty years or so, globalization has resulted in an astonishing rise in the power of place-less leaders, meaning decision makers who are unconcerned about the impact of their decisions on communities living in particular places. The rise in place-less power and, in particular, the growth of multinational companies driven by profit-seeking motives, is a root cause not just of this global pandemic, but also the present climate catastrophe. Fortunately, there are many ways of modifying the behaviour of place-less decision makers.

Harnessing the collective power of investors and employees

First, people working for these multinational companies, as well as those who invest in them, can push for more responsible approaches to capitalism. For example, campaigns to encourage companies to advance social and environmental goals, not just financial return, should be supported.

Trade unions are, of course, already active in arguing for all businesses to adopt a more farsighted approach. Some business leaders appear to understand that their success as a business requires them to change in a more socially aware direction. However, the track record of most major companies remains poor.

John Elkington advocated the idea of 'triple bottom line' leadership in 1997.[7] His suggestion was that forward-looking businesses should measure their performance against three criteria – economic prosperity, environmental quality and social justice – not just the economic. Over twenty years later, we now know that few big companies have moved in this direction, and the idea that any of them are giving equal weight to these three criteria seems far-fetched.

Regulating big tech companies

To make progress, it is clear that nation states, ideally acting together, must take steps to regulate place-less power. It is extraordinary that so little progress has been made on introducing a digital tax on big tech companies. For example, Amazon paid a total of £220 million in direct taxes in the UK in 2018, despite its total revenues in the country amounting to £10.9 billion.[8] It is not difficult to see why so many high street shops across the country are boarded up. Retailers in towns, cities and villages have been exposed to years of unfair competition from multinational companies that make strenuous efforts to actively avoid contributing properly to the public purse.

Margaret Hodge MP, when she was Chair of the UK Public Accounts Committee, exposed the extraordinary extent of tax avoidance being practised by big multinational companies. Her book records breathtaking exchanges between her Committee and the chief executive officers of, for example, Google, Starbucks and Amazon.[9] The Committee's investigations showed that all these place-less companies constructed fiendishly complex webs of companies for no other commercial purpose than to avoid paying a fair rate of tax in the countries where they do business. These avoidance arrangements are so complex that, under questioning, some of these business leaders admitted that they did not understand them – only their lawyers could explain what they were doing.

This is an unacceptable state of affairs. The worry is that things are going to get worse, if national governments fail to act. The big tech companies are already positioning themselves to take advantage of the COVID-19 pandemic, to expand surveillance and data mining, by gaining access to huge amounts of personal data currently held by government departments.[10]

Expanding place-based power

The third way of reining in irresponsible place-less power is to expand place-based power. In Chapter Six, I provide an 'innovation cameo' of Freiburg, a small, innovative city in southern Germany. All local authorities in Germany enjoy constitutional protection. This means that the rights of localities to govern themselves is enshrined in the constitution of the state and that, as a result, local authorities have substantial autonomy to do what they think is right for their communities. The City of Freiburg owns lots of land in and around the city so that, as development takes place, the massive uplift in land values accrues to the public purse. Martin Horn, Mayor of Freiburg, has recently decided that future housing development in the city must ensure that 50 per cent of the housing units are genuinely affordable. The beauty of these arrangements is that local leaders are able to stop place-less power exploiting the people of Freiburg. Investors and developers must either comply with the social and environmental objectives set down by the city, or go elsewhere.

It is important to stress that Germany is not unique in recognizing the value of having powerful and effective local government. Other countries also ensure that local authorities have constitutional protection from a potentially overbearing central state and, in many countries, local authorities have far more fiscal autonomy than those in the UK.

Elsewhere, I have suggested that local/central relations in the UK have been travelling in precisely the wrong direction for at least ten years. Instead of devolving substantial power to local government, the Conservative government has, particularly in England, hidden moves to super-centralize the state behind a smokescreen of 'devolution deal' rhetoric.[11]

The three key tests of meaningful devolution to elected local authorities are: constitutional protection; a substantial range of functions; and significant local tax-raising powers. Local government systems with these characteristics have the freedom to do things differently, and this bolsters the innovative capacity of a society. As well as being more democratic, it provides the means for the emergence of new ideas that can then compete for wider acceptance.

The need for a constitutional convention in the UK

What do citizens think about the relative merits of local and central government? In the UK, it has long been established that citizens trust local government more than central government. Since the COVID-19 outbreak, positive public opinions towards local government have soared even further ahead. In June 2020, opinion survey findings relating to England indicated that 73 per cent of citizens said they trust their council to make decisions about how services are provided in their area, compared with 18 per cent who said they trusted central government.[12]

Public opinion, as well as academic analysis, suggests that a radical rebalancing of power between elected local authorities and central government in the UK is long overdue. A good way to achieve this would be to set up an independent constitutional convention, to examine the way power has been removed from localities over the years, and to set out bold proposals to rebalance the local/central power structure of the country.

In early 2016, the English Local Government Association (LGA) invited the author to prepare an international review of sub-national governance in other countries. The aim of that study was to widen the conversation about devolution in the UK, by examining sub-national models of governance found elsewhere. In order to guide the study, I asked the senior political leaders commissioning the work to help identify principles of good governance that could then guide the research.[13] The political leaders agreed six principles, and I summarize them here:

- *Civic leadership:* Does the governance model provide effective place-based leadership?
- *Effective decision making:* Does the model support high-quality decision-making processes that go beyond discovering the preferences of various stakeholders?
- *Transparency and efficiency:* Does the model make it clear who is making decisions, on what issues, when, why and how?
- *Accountability:* Does the model ensure that decision makers are held to account?

- *Public involvement:* Does the model provide for effective public involvement in decision making?
- *Business engagement:* Does the model provide for the effective involvement of local business interests?

These principles were used in the study to evaluate various respected examples of sub-national governance. They could, perhaps, provide a helpful input into the work of a constitutional convention, should one be set up. Another useful contribution to the debate about how to rebalance power in Britain is provided by the LGA report *Re-thinking Local.*[14]

Place-based planning for a post COVID-19 future

In Chapter One, I noted that the disaster studies literature suggests that cities and localities that look ahead, develop a far-sighted vision for their area and have firm strategic plans in place are far better placed to respond to a crisis. But what do such plans look like? First, good plans will need to be holistic in nature, and will need to be guided by the key value of caring for people and the planet (as set out earlier). This is not an altogether daunting challenge, as city and regional planners across the world have been active in developing plans along these lines in recent years.

This is certainly the case in the UK. A 2020 research report, *Plan the World We Need*, from the Royal Town Planning Institute provides a useful set of suggestions on how to go about doing this.[15] The subtitle of this report is 'The contribution of planning to sustainable, resilient and inclusive recovery'. The study explains how sound planning can accelerate progress towards a zero-carbon economy, as well as helping to tackle social inequality, reshape transport priorities and promote an expansion of green industry jobs.

Another useful policy contribution is provided by the final report of the UK2070 Commission, *Make No Little Plans.*[16]

Published in early 2020 just before the COVID-19 pandemic hit the UK, it puts the spotlight on regional inequalities in Britain, provides a national analysis of the challenges facing the UK, and sets out a ten-point action plan. These action points include developing a national spatial plan for England, and implementing proposals for a strengthened approach to devolution in England.

As explained in Chapter Five, Bristol has, in the period since 2016, developed an ambitious One City Plan. Those involved in the Bristol effort have learned from innovative cities in other countries. In particular, the Bristol City Office team drew insights from the One NYC plan, developed by New York City.[17] The good news is that many cities in a wide range of countries are moving in the direction of holistic place-based planning, and this is encouraging. Three features of the Bristol approach are noteworthy.

- First, a Bristol One City Approach underpins the Bristol One City Plan.[18] The collaborative model of governing that has been developed in Bristol provides the civic infrastructure to ensure that the plan has systemic buy-in from all key stakeholders, to ensure that it will be delivered.
- Second, the Bristol One City Plan takes detailed and explicit account of the UN's SDGs.
- Third, the process is unusually inclusive, with regular City Gatherings and six thematic boards actively consulting on the six major themes in the plan. There is, then, an ongoing commitment to amplify citizen voice in the decision-making processes that shape the One City Plan, and there is a public commitment to review the plan on an annual basis.

The potential of New Civic Leadership

The New Civic Leadership conceptual framework, set out in Chapter Four, is intended not only to enhance understanding of place-based leadership, but also to provide practical suggestions on how to improve the quality and effectiveness of local collaborative leadership. The central claim is that, within most localities, there are likely to be five overlapping realms of place-based leadership – see Figure 4.2. These are: political leadership; public managerial/professional leadership; community leadership; business leadership; and trade union leadership. The overlaps between these realms can, with the right kind of overall civic leadership, become powerful innovation zones – meaning spaces within which actors can co-create new ways of thinking and new solutions. The New Civic Leadership model has been applied in Bristol since 2016, and Chapter Five provides an account of how this collaborative approach to governance has worked in practice.

By drawing on my experience of using the New Civic Leadership framework in the UK and abroad, I offer, in this section, three suggestions designed to advance scholarship in the fields of leadership studies, public policy, political science, public management and innovation studies in general.

First, it is clear that place is not receiving the attention it deserves in these fields. I agree with Brad Jackson, who claims that:

> The importance of place and place leadership is often acknowledged but rarely becomes the focal point for public leadership researchers who have tended to be interested in creating more generalisable theories that are determinedly not tied to place ... By contrast, I am convinced that place is too important a component of leadership to be side-lined in this manner.[19]

Jackson's comments relate to leadership studies, but they apply just as well to public management and public policy more generally. Taking explicit account of place, and the distinctiveness of places, can improve scholarship by, literally, bringing it 'down to earth' and connecting it more directly to the lived experience of actors on the ground.

Second, can we encourage more research and analysis of 'civic' leadership? In modern societies, we certainly need to improve public leadership as well as private sector leadership. That goes without saying. But, it is worth asking whether these public/private distinctions need some reconsideration. There has been a welcome rise in social entrepreneurship in recent years, with many social businesses now blending for-profit objectives with social and environmental purposes. In Bristol, as I mentioned earlier, the City Office has developed a range of place-based leadership programmes that attract participants from the public, private and non-profit sectors. These efforts are designed to improve civic leadership, not just public and private leadership. Putting the spotlight on the 'civic' dimension can help leadership studies to expand the notion of caring leadership beyond caring for employees to outward-facing caring for people and the planet.

Third, the New Civic Leadership framework is intended to assist civic leaders to step beyond improvement as an aim, to embrace bold innovation. In our modern, turbulent world, we need to strengthen our civic capacity to innovate as never before. Doing more of the same plus a bit of improvement is not going to cut it. The framework suggests that civic leaders should actively create innovation zones – spaces that convene actors from the five realms of place-based leadership. This strategy can bring together people with different perspectives and experiences and, with the right leadership, these new constellations can co-create entirely new ways of seeing and acting.[20] Successful civic innovation stems, then, from a discovery process that, while it draws inspiration from any amount of sources beyond a place, is rooted in the life and culture of communities living in particular places. This insight can enhance the quality of scholarship on innovation. It implies a radical shift away from *smart* cities towards *wise* cities.[21]

The co-creation of a caring society

Can the shock of the COVID-19 pandemic open our eyes to new possibilities? Will the societal impact of the disease prompt serious questions to be raised about future possibilities? The pandemic has certainly jolted our world, and there will be more pandemics in the future. If we want to protect ourselves against further disasters, if we want to promote fairness in society, support human flourishing and defeat the threat of global warming, there can be 'no going back'. But where should we go?

In Chapter Three, I shared some ideas on the changing relationships between the state, the market and civil society and, also, on the interplay between the individual, nature and society. The argument presented in that chapter is that, to develop sound and coherent policies for a post COVID-19 world, societies will need to consider afresh the core values that they want to see guiding the way we live in the new world that we will be co-creating. In an effort to enlighten this conversation, I have suggested that the political window of possibilities should be shifted towards caring for people and the planet – see Figure 3.3. This will not be a trouble-free journey. It means *not* going in the opposite direction of promoting unregulated markets and rampant individualism. Powerful vested interests will, to be sure, oppose such a shift.

A key insight from this discussion is that, contrary to neo-liberal dogma, expanding the role of the state can *strengthen our freedom*. Without strong, wise and compassionate nation states, our freedom from disease and suffering cannot be delivered. Place-less power will continue to exploit places, people and nature, unless we develop a vision of a society that really does care for people and the planet.

Joan Tronto, a professor of political science, has provided an extended presentation of what a caring democracy might look like. She notes that:

> A truly just society does not use the market to hide current and past injustices. The purpose of economic life

is to support care, not the other way around. Production is not an end in itself, it is a means to the end of living as well as we can. And in a democratic society, this means everyone can live well, not just the few.[22]

In Chapter Three, I offered a statement of progressive values that could guide the co-creation of a caring society. In addition to caring for others and animals, as articulated by Tronto, I add in, explicitly, caring for the natural environment on which we all depend. My suggestion is that a progressive society is, then, an inclusive society – it is characterized by a participatory approach to decision making and aims to advance social, economic and environmental justice.

Conclusions

A central claim of this book is that local people living in particular communities and localities are key drivers of societal change. During the COVID-19 pandemic, the power of place-based caring and collaboration has been highly visible across the world. Human kindness to neighbours and strangers has flourished, as has local civic leadership.

However, in too many countries, national governments do not appreciate or value place-based knowledge and action. In addition, we have seen the power of place, the power of communities living in particular localities, diminished by the growth of, what I call, 'place-less power'. Place-less decision makers are to be found in multinational companies, where decisions are often driven by narrow calculations relating to the growth of private profit rather than any broader societal purpose, and in distant central government departments, where too many politicians seek to play places off against each other.

The key challenge for post COVID-19 strategy is to recognize that we need to develop much more effective arrangements for anticipating and coping with complex threats – of whatever kind. This means improving the way we govern ourselves and, in particular, strengthening the power of place-based local democracy. Enhancing place-based power and influence is critical, as it builds societal resilience.

Back in 1762, as explained in Chapter Four, Jean-Jacques Rousseau recognized the importance of creating inclusive forms of government to serve public purpose.[23] Michael Sandel builds on Rousseau's arguments and provides a robust critique of the way we have allowed markets and market thinking, rather than civic purpose, to penetrate spheres of life where they don't belong. Sandel explains how financial incentives and other market mechanisms crowd out other important values, like generosity, solidarity, caring for others and caring for the planet.[24]

An uplifting feature of the way communities have responded to the COVID-19 challenge has been the spectacular expansion of self-organizing community groups working at neighbourhood level to help the vulnerable and needy. The evidence suggests that massive numbers of people are not at all driven by the pursuit of private self-interest. This is not an accident. This compassionate behaviour is entirely consistent with recent studies of human nature, notably *Humankind*, the magisterial analysis provided by Rutger Bregman.[25]

Sandel is right, when he argues that economistic thinking lacks understanding of human virtue:

> Altruism, generosity, solidarity, and civic spirit are not like commodities that are depleted with use. They are more like muscles that develop and grow stronger with exercise. One of the defects of a market-driven society is that it lets these virtues languish. To renew our public life we need to exercise them more strenuously.[26]

Now is the time for those of us who care about people and the planet to flex those muscles.

Notes

[1] Honigsbaum M. (2020) *The Pandemic Century: A history of global contagion from the Spanish flu to COVID-19*, London: Penguin.

[2] Wallace R. (2016) *Big Farms Make Big Flu*, New York: Monthly Review Press.

[3] Bregman R. (2020) *Humankind: A hopeful history*, London: Bloomsbury Publishing.

[4] I draw this idea of developing a grammar, or series of grammars, from Cooper D. (1976) *The Grammar of Living: An examination of political acts*. Harmondsworth: Penguin.

[5] Lukes S. (2005) *Power: A radical view* (2nd edn), Basingstoke: Palgrave.

[6] Williamson J. (2020) *A Better recovery: Learning the lessons of the corona crisis to create a stronger, fairer economy*, May, London: TUC. https://www.tuc.org.uk/ABetterRecovery?page=1

[7] Elkington J. (1997) *Cannibals with Forks: The triple bottom line of 21st century business*, Oxford: Capstone Publishing Limited.

[8] Armstrong A. (2019) 'Amazon pays £220m tax on British revenue of £10.9 billion', *The Times*, 4 September.

[9] Hodge M. (2016) *Called to Account: How corporate bad behaviour and government waste combine to cost us millions*, London: Little Brown. See, in particular, Chapter 5: 'The tax tricks of Google, Starbucks and Amazon', pp 75–107.

[10] Klein N. (2020) 'How big tech plans to profit from the pandemic', *The Guardian*, 19 May.

[11] Hambleton R. (2017) 'The super-centralisation of the English state – Why we need to move beyond the devolution deception', *Local Economy*, 32(1): 3–13.

[12] Local Government Association (2020) *Polling on Resident Satisfaction with Councils: Round 26*, June, London: Local Government Association.

[13] Hambleton R. (2016) *English Devolution: Learning lessons from international models of sub-national governance: A research report*, London: Local Government Association. https://www.local.gov.uk/english-devolution-learning-lessons-international-models-sub-national-governance

[14] Local Government Association (2020) *Re-thinking Local*, June, London: Local Government Association. https://www.local.gov.uk/sites/default/files/documents/3.70%20Rethinking%20local_%23councilscan_landscape_FINAL.pdf

[15] Royal Town Planning Institute (RTPI) (2020) *Plan The World We Need*. Research Paper, June, London: RTPI. https://www.rtpi.org.uk/news/plan-the-world-we-need/

[16] UK2070 Commission (2020) *Make No Little Plans: Acting at scale for a fairer and stronger future*, Final Report, February, London: UK2070

Commission. http://uk2070.org.uk/wp-content/uploads/2020/02/UK2070-FINAL-REPORT.pdf

[17] New York City (2019) *One NYC: Building a strong and fair city*, April, New York: City of New York. http://onenyc.cityofnewyork.us/reports-resources/

[18] The Bristol One City Plan was launched in January 2019 and is rolled forward annually. https://www.bristolonecity.com

[19] Jackson B. (2019) 'The power of place in public leadership research and development', *International Journal of Public Leadership*, 15(4): 209–233.

[20] I discuss the leadership of innovation in more detail in Hambleton R. (2015) *Leading the Inclusive City: Place-based innovation for a bounded planet*, Bristol: Policy Press, pp 139–171.

[21] For those interested in more detail on the 'From smart cities to wise cities' argument see: Hambleton (2015 pp 283–307) (Note 20).

[22] Tronto J.C. (2013) *Caring Democracy: Markets, equality and justice*, New York: New York University Press, p 170.

[23] Jean-Jacques Rousseau (1762) *The Social Contract*, trans. Cranston M. (1968) *Rousseau: The Social Contract*, London: Penguin.

[24] Sandel M.J. (2012) *What Money Can't Buy: The moral limits of markets*, London: Allen Lane.

[25] Bregman R. (2020) (see Note 3).

[26] Sandel M.J. (2012 p 130) (see Note 24).

Index